Maimonides

Classic Thinkers

Richard T. W. Arthur, *Leibniz*

Terrell Carver, *Marx*

Daniel Davies, *Maimonides*

Daniel E. Flage, *Berkeley*

J. M. Fritzman, *Hegel*

Bernard Gert, *Hobbes*

Thomas Kemple, *Simmel*

Ralph McInerny, *Aquinas*

Dale E. Miller, *J. S. Mill*

Joanne Paul, *Thomas More*

William J. Prior, *Socrates*

A. J. Pyle, *Locke*

Michael Quinn, *Bentham*

James T. Schleifer, *Tocqueville*

Craig Smith, *Adam Smith*

Céline Spector, *Rousseau*

Justin Steinberg and Valtteri Viljanen, *Spinoza*

Andrew Ward, *Kant*

Maimonides

Daniel Davies

polity

To my father, Jonathan, and in memory of my mother, Lillian.

First published in 2024 by Polity Press

Polity Press
65 Bridge Street
Cambridge CB2 1UR, UK

Polity Press
111 River Street
Hoboken, NJ 07030, USA

ISBN-13: 978-1-5095-2290-3 (hardback)
ISBN-13: 978-1-5095-2291-0 (paperback)

A catalogue record for this book is available from the British Library.

Library of Congress Control Number: 2023938503

Typeset in 10.5 on 12pt Palatino
by Fakenham Prepress Solutions, Fakenham, Norfolk NR21 8NL
Printed and bound by CPI Group (UK) Ltd, Croydon, CR0 4YY

The publisher has used its best endeavours to ensure that the URLs for external websites referred to in this book are correct and active at the time of going to press. However, the publisher has no responsibility for the websites and can make no guarantee that a site will remain live or that the content is or will remain appropriate.

Every effort has been made to trace all copyright holders, but if any have been overlooked the publisher will be pleased to include any necessary credits in any subsequent reprint or edition.

For further information on Polity, visit our website:
politybooks.com

Contents

Acknowledgements

When George Owers first suggested writing an introduction to Maimonides, I wondered whether such a book was really necessary. I then thought about my own initiations into medieval philosophy, much of which came through teachers who had little or no connection with Maimonides studies or Jewish philosophy but focused on Arabic–Islamic or Latin thought. The same is true of my attempts to delve deeper, so my perspective on Maimonides is not only informed by existing works about him and, on reflection, I concluded that there is indeed a place for a philosophical introduction to be added to the literature about one of the most discussed Jewish philosophers, and I have tried to channel the kinds of lessons that I found helpful. I would never even have considered writing this book had George not asked, so I thank him for the initiative. I also appreciate his patience, as well as that of other editors at Polity Press, Julia Davies, Ian Malcolm, Ellen MacDonald-Kramer and Susan Beer, as the project took longer than initially envisaged.

I am grateful to a number of people who have offered personal support while the book was gestating. I'd like to mention in particular Merav Rosenfeld Hadad, Racheli Haliva, José Liht and George Wilkes. George also commented on versions of the chapters as I completed them, and I am indebted to Charles Manekin for commenting on a draft of the entire book, and the referees for Polity, who made some very helpful remarks.

I am fortunate to have a concerned and supportive family and am thankful for their ongoing encouragement, especially through some recent upheavals. Without exception, Dad and Hilary, my aunt and uncle, my siblings and their own families (including Lia, who wasn't around last time), all deserve special thanks and appreciation, for behaviour and character.

Finally, Adam and Nira, together with Gloria and Stuart, have created an environment that enabled me to write this book, and I am especially grateful to them.

1

Biography and Introduction

Every evening, Moses Maimonides travelled from the Sultan's residence in Cairo back to his home in Fusṭāṭ. After a long day ministering as physician at the palace, he arrived to a crowd of patients demanding attention. Before he could see them, he needed to excuse himself and eat his single daily meal. By the day's end, he was so exhausted that he was unable even to speak. Such, at least, is the report he sends in a letter written late in his life. By this point, Maimonides had already completed the major philosophical and religious works for which he is now renowned, and his reputation had spread throughout the Jewish world, both in the Arabic-speaking lands in which he spent his days and among the Jews living under Christian rule. Many details are known of Maimonides' eventful, at times turbulent, life. As befits a revered religious leader, there are reports about him, some of which are fictitious or exaggerated, but information can also be gleaned from his surviving correspondence. Some of his letters were passed down, and even translated into Hebrew, as independent treatises. Others have been found in a trove of documents discovered in Cairo. We learn a great deal about his life, character and thought from these sources.

Like many of his philosophical contemporaries, Maimonides made his living as a medical doctor. The royal court he attended belonged to the famous Saladin. There he met other scholars and well-known dignitaries, and wrote important medical treatises. For a time, he was the community's figurehead, 'the head of the Jews', and in this capacity acted as a representative and mediator between the Jewish community and the governmental authorities. The role came with responsibility for many everyday community affairs as well and he bemoaned the demands on his time that kept him from studying and dedicating himself to striving for true human fulfilment: 'the great things and high offices that Jews attain in our time are not in my eyes happiness and perfect goodness worth striving for, and not, by the exalted God's life, a minor evil but an appalling vexation and burden. For the perfect man who attains ultimate happiness is the one who attends to the refinement of his religious life, carrying out his obligations and avoiding the evil of all people.'[1]

One of the more famous of his letters, although some question its authenticity, is addressed to the community of Jews living under Almohad rule in parts of North Africa and Spain; it is known as *The Epistle on Religious Persecution*. The author advises Jews in provinces conquered by the Almohads to convert outwardly to Islam, in order to save their lives, while continuing to practise Judaism in private and making every effort to leave for a more welcoming domain as soon as possible, because the rulers forced many, including other Muslims, to accept their own interpretation of Islam. He explains that the conversion the Almohads demand involves very light conditions. According to the letter's report, it was enough simply to recite the *shahāda*, to verbally profess Islam, in order to undergo the conversion itself. Moreover, while rabbinic Judaism considers idolatry to be a cardinal sin that should not be transgressed even on pain of death, it does not consider Islam idolatrous, so conversion is preferable to perishing. Forced converts would also not have been engaging in idolatry by attending mosque services. Since Maimonides passed through Almohad territory, he might have been among those forced to behave as if they had converted. The historian al-Qiftī, who was a contemporary of Maimonides, reported that he did in fact do so. The story goes that he was recognised in Egypt by someone who had known him years before, when he had been living as a Muslim in a different land. Maimonides was reported to the authorities and left open to the charge of apostasy. However, the judge ruled that a forced conversion is no conversion at all and the charges were dismissed. Some historians consider the extant version of al-Qiftī's text to be unreliable, and the account of Maimonides' conversion to be no more than an unproven tale. In support, it is claimed that there was no general campaign to convert absolutely everyone by the sword, even though there was widespread persecution, so there is no strong reason to credit the claim that Maimonides must himself have converted. One of the various reasons the letter on persecution is sometimes considered a misattribution, although not one of the main reasons, lies in the fact that there are passages that might indicate that the author had himself done exactly this. As some argue that there is no evidence that Maimonides did actually convert, they can claim that he would not have written a letter implying that he had done so. It is then argued that this letter therefore cannot be by Maimonides. There are many spurious works attributed to him; a great name is often borrowed to lend authority to works written by unknown authors.[2]

Whether or not the letter is genuine, it illustrates that a part of Maimonides' life was lived under oppressive conditions quite different from those he later experienced in Egypt. Maimonides had been forced to flee his homeland at an early age. He was born in Cordoba in 1137/8 CE and travelled with his family through the Almohad heartlands in Morocco to the Levant. He also knew personal tragedy. In a letter addressed to someone he had met during his stay in Acre, prior to his arrival in Egypt, he mentions how badly he had been affected by his brother David's death. For an entire year, he reports, he was consumed with fever and unable to move from his bed. David had been a merchant trading in precious stones, before he drowned in the Indian Ocean during a commercial venture, and Maimonides indicates that his younger brother's activities had allowed him to feel secure in his dedication to study. Although he had already studied medicine, he may have practised it as a serious profession only after being forced to do so in order to support himself and the family that David left behind.

In spite of his responsibilities and his need for remuneration, Maimonides' literary output was impressive. When in Egypt, he completed a running commentary on the Mishnah, the first of its kind, which explained in Arabic the discussions at the foundation of the rabbinic oral law, thereby making it accessible to Jews with various education levels. He also compiled a law code known as the *Mishneh Torah*, 'the repetition of the Torah', which was unparalleled by any previous rabbinic text in scope and conception. It contains an account of the entire oral law, as Maimonides saw it, so that people would no longer need to wade through the plethora of discussions and judgements that had accrued over the centuries in order to make practical decisions. Rather than the Aramaic of the Talmud, known only to scholars, he chose to write the *Code* in Hebrew, taking the Mishnah's language as his model. He explained that biblical Hebrew was too limited for the purpose, and that the Mishnah is easy to understand. In this he was breaking new ground. His language is remarkably clear and elegant and remains, perhaps, the best example of eloquent Hebrew in a comprehensive rabbinic law code.

The *Code* became known as the *yad ḥazaqa*, 'the mighty hand', an allusion to the Pentateuch's final verse: 'and for all the mighty hand and for all the great awesomeness that Moses did in the sight of all Israel'. Through his law code, Moses Maimonides was likened to his namesake, the original lawgiver himself. 'From Moses until Moses there was none like Moses.' This is a famous saying credited to Jonathan of Lunel. Jonathan sent queries about the *Code* that seem to have particularly impressed its author. These questions arrived later in Maimonides' life and, in response, he lamented not having noted down his sources, as doing so would have made it easier to respond to questions and criticisms. Even though he aimed to encompass the whole of the law, he recognised that his code would not be perfect, so he invited scholars to compare it to earlier rulings in order to make sure it was sound and to iron out confusions and ambiguities. He replied to Jonathan and to another letter from the sages of Lunel, in Southern France, finding hope in the dedication they displayed to Torah and Talmud study, which he claims has almost disappeared from the communities in the Arab world. Now, he writes, the Jews in non-Arabic countries are ready to take over the mantle from those in the East. 'There remains no one in support of our Torah except you, my redeeming brethren. Be therefore strong and fortify yourselves for the sake of our people and our God.' Such a despondent appraisal of Arabic Judaism's decline may have been exaggerated on purpose and may perhaps have been a rhetorical way to encourage the growing European Jewish community living outside the Islamicate to embrace a philosophical Judaism. Or maybe motivation came from feeling bruised by criticism he received from some in the Baghdadi Jewish community, or by the persecution of the Jews of Yemen, whom, in a poignant epistle, he encouraged to stand by their faith despite their travails.

At the time, the law code more than any other work made Maimonides' name and it has also ensured his exalted place in the Jewish tradition. Because people wanted to read his other books, Maimonides' work as a whole did much to spread Hebrew philosophy by giving impetus to a translation movement from Arabic that had only recently begun. As well as sending particular questions about the *Mishneh Torah*, the Lunel sages asked Maimonides to translate into Hebrew the works he had written in Arabic, the everyday language of most Jews and the language in which almost all Jewish philosophy had been written until then, which was not generally spoken by the Jews of Provence. Chief among them was the *Guide for the Perplexed*. Maimonides himself had no time to do so, but agreed that one of their own, Samuel Ibn Tibbon (d. 1232), would be a good person to undertake the task. Together with other members of his family, Ibn Tibbon translated many great works of Judaeo-Arabic philosophy, which have now become classics of the Hebrew Jewish tradition in their Tibbonite versions. In order to aid their readers, the Tibbonites also translated other central works of Graeco-Arabic and Islamic philosophy and wrote independent exegetical and philosophical works. Their translations and commentaries established a Hebrew philosophical tradition and their linguistic choices permeated later Hebrew writings of many different sorts.

Maimonides' name is well known to historians of general philosophy. He was introduced to the Christian Scholastic world in Latin translation only shortly after he wrote the *Guide*, allowing for Aquinas' appreciative references and respectful criticisms of some of his arguments. While his name is noted in histories of Western philosophy, it towers over the history of Jewish thought, indeed of Judaism as a whole. His importance stems from the fame he acquired during his lifetime but also from the myriad ways in which his books have been employed ever since. In a recent study, one scholar explains that 'every path in Jewish thought and law from the twelfth century on bears some of Maimonides' imprint'.[3] Despite his reputation and influence, the main achievements of his philosophical works consist in the use he made of philosophy, rather than novel contributions to the classical philosophical fields, such as logic, natural science, metaphysics and ethics. Most, if not all, would agree that he was the medieval Jewish philosopher to have exercised the greatest direct influence on the Jewish tradition, but some dissent from the claim that he was the greatest medieval Jewish philosopher, qua philosopher. However, rating philosophers is a strange business, and originality can be measured in different ways. Besides, who is qualified to undertake such an appraisal? Maimonides is not only a highly influential medieval Jewish thinker; he is also original in his scope and application, and his philosophy is worth studying in its own right.

Many who read Maimonides do so through their own contemporary lenses, a practice that is not only legitimate but might be true to Maimonides' own vision. He is the teacher extraordinaire, as well as an inspiration for ongoing critical engagement with the tradition. Among his major interpreters, some of the most important find in his work the seeds of their own philosophical and theological struggles and concerns. He is often a stimulus for creative Jewish theology and philosophy. This is true of many academic students of Maimonides too. In this book, I would like to introduce Maimonides' philosophy through discussions of the major issues that exercise scholars in studies of medieval philosophy generally. However, the Jewish component of his works cannot be ignored. Indeed, almost all the Maimonidean texts mentioned in this introduction are first and foremost Jewish texts, inasmuch as they are concerned primarily with issues arising from religion, and the Jewish religion in particular. These works make heavy use of philosophy. They are no less philosophical than Jewish. Against Maimonides' historical background, one can see that attributing a distinction between philosophy and religion to his own self-perception is artificial, even though it has now become commonplace to say that they oppose one another. Maimonides considered engaging in philosophy necessary for a fulfilling life, for a life that is truly human, but also as itself a form of worshipping God.

In view of the biography sketched above, albeit extremely brief and selective, there is hardly a need to justify saying that Maimonides was a Jewish philosopher. But the very notion of 'Jewish Philosophy' is contested. Is there really any such thing? What would make a philosophy particularly Jewish? One reasonable answer emphasises the sources used. Maimonides constantly draws on biblical and rabbinic sources and expresses his ideas through them. One could also consider the way in which he integrated philosophical ideas into his conception of Judaism and the halakha, the Jewish law, by, for example, making them the guiding principles of the *Mishneh Torah*. These are relevant if we are not to lose sight of the Jewish aspect, which could be possible because the content of many of the discussions focused on in this book is written in conversation with philosophers who are not Jewish, but pagan or Muslim. I would like to suggest that one should also consider Maimonides' target audience and the way in which he tried to influence them. His religious and philosophical works were not aimed at a universal readership but specifically at Jews. Even the Arabic ones were written in Hebrew characters, as was common practice among Arabic-speaking Jews, and aimed at a Jewish readership. His concern in these works was always to influence the contemporary community and advance his interpretation of the tradition. Maimonides seemed to consider himself at a crossroads. He was both continuing an old Jewish tradition, but also updating it for a new time. Some of the ways in which he set about doing so were truly profound, even if the philosophical worldview he expounded can be found in earlier Jewish thinkers too. Maimonides' commitment to community and the rabbinic tradition could not have been stronger, and I think that someone can be considered to engage in 'Jewish Philosophy' when the aim is to address the living Jewish community, whether that is reflected in the language and proof texts used or the desire to exert influence. Even so, Maimonides' views deserve attention outside of their time and religious environment, and to them I now turn.

The first main chapters will deal with matters of humanity. Maimonides' view of human nature stands squarely in the Arabic Aristotelian tradition, inasmuch as he considers humans to be 'rational animals' and human perfection to consist in acquiring the moral and rational virtues. Chapter 2 explains Maimonides' view of the soul, human nature, and the difference between humans and other animals. It also introduces and explains some basic philosophical and scientific ideas that serve as background to understanding both the ideas in the chapter and in the rest of the book. Asking what it means to be a good human involves ethical questions about behaviour and, in this context, the purpose of halakha also needs to be discussed briefly.

Maimonides was also part of a theological tradition, and theology presented a corrective to the overconfidence he thought some had in a number of Aristotelian doctrines. Consequently, even though Maimonides' teachings are in line with the philosophers' virtue ethics and psychological theories, he adopts an uncompromising theocentric viewpoint that demands humility not only on an individual level but towards the whole cosmos and, ultimately, towards the divine. This attitude is manifest in his response to the theoretical difficulties motivated by evil and suffering. The question of evil is the topic of Chapter 3, which also deals with divine providence and God's knowledge. Maimonides' response to the problem of evil can be seen as a critique of the problem itself. Together with many others in the Western philosophical tradition, Maimonides claimed that evil is a privation. He is somewhat unusual in emphasis, however, because his explanation does not exactly lead to a theodicy. Instead, he argues that there is no good reason for us to think that we ought not to suffer. Nor does he limit God's knowledge. Those who argue that the presence of evil indicates God's ignorance of individuals or impotence over their circumstances presume to know what God's purpose in creating is, and ultimately judge the whole of creation from the perspective of humanity. In Maimonides' view, people are not the purpose of God's creating, so this is a fundamental misunderstanding. Rather than limiting God's knowledge, he argues that God's providence is limited. It is unusual to distinguish them in such a way. Not attending to the distinction has often led scholars to think that Maimonides' position on providence is particularly obscure and riddled with contradictions. It can be seen to cohere, though, if his theocentric statements are taken into account. He argues that the presence of evil in the world does not show God to be ignorant. Instead, it shows that humans are not as important as they might think.

Maimonides' arguments about God's knowledge and providence reflect the limits that he draws around human knowledge, which is a theme running through Chapters 4, 5, and 6, as they deal with theological issues from which these limitations are most easily identified. So, while the previous chapters contain much about human nature, the next three chapters are concerned more with what we can know about divine matters, if anything. Chapter 4 considers creation and the relationship between God and the world. Maimonides' discussion revolves around the question of whether or not the world had a beginning, which is sometimes considered to be different from the question of whether the world depends on God for its existence. His treatment limits the scope of human knowledge, since he argues that it is impossible to know for certain either way. Many of his arguments are directed against those who reject creation, and he tries to show that they cannot demonstrate that their view is true. A demonstration is a very strong kind of proof that would be accepted by anybody who understands it properly. In the absence of such a proof, Maimonides says that either the topic remains a problem or one of the opinions is believed even though reason cannot adjudicate for certain which is true. It is therefore necessary to understand why creation cannot be understood along the lines of the kinds of generation that occur in the world in order to see why the arguments against creation fail. However, Maimonides does not stop there. He argues that there are reasons to believe that the world did have a beginning, even though such a beginning can be neither conceived nor imagined. Understanding his arguments requires some background in Aristotelian dialectic and the role it plays in the *Guide* and, in this chapter, I will say a little about the *Guide's* dialectical nature.

Chapters 5 and 6 are dedicated to God's existence and attributes. Chapter 5 considers what Maimonides says about belief generally and the upshots of his arguments for God's existence. It also explains and discusses some of those arguments, which are difficult in themselves but made more so by the fact that Maimonides presents them in succinct fashion. His arguments for God conclude that God is identical with a 'necessarily existing being'. Chapter 6 explores what this claim can mean and explains the consequences that Maimonides draws out concerning divine attributes and religious language. Both 5 and 6 contain material that is somewhat more technical than previous chapters, but that is fitting for the topic, which was considered to be an advanced subject to be studied in depth only after sufficiently grasping other fields. Since the concept of a necessary existent has often been called into question, and is generally unpopular in modern philosophy, I deemed it apposite, in order to clarify what lies behind Maimonides' claims, to address some of the issues surrounding it that seem to pose problems. Chapter 6 therefore enters into a philosophical analysis that draws on current debates in analytic philosophy. Such tools are not often put to use in studies of Maimonides, or of medieval Jewish philosophy generally. I have therefore divided the chapter into two parts. Some readers might wish to skim or skip the second part, which deals with these metaphysical concerns, and focus instead on the discussion of negative theology, which requires less elaboration from outside Maimonides' own text.

All of the topics I discuss in this book are subject to dispute in the secondary literature and have been for centuries. As with many great thinkers, there are disagreements concerning what his arguments mean and how they ought to be interpreted. Since this book focuses mainly on explaining the philosophical background and offering an interpretation of its own, I will not survey all the alternative under-standings but I will mention some of the more notable positions as the need arises. In any case, there are other works that can be consulted for precisely this purpose. Given the confines of an intro-ductory book, I have also been unable to enter into as much detail about some of the issues as I would have liked. For both of these reasons, I have included a brief list of recommended reading at the end to guide readers who wish to investigate further. Maimonides' work and thought covers so many different topics and has so many different facets; I had to be somewhat selective and chose to concentrate on matters of universal concern that continue to be discussed both by philosophers and theologians today, as well as by scholars who work on other great philosophers of Maimonides' time.

The closing chapter provides a brief overview of Maimonides' reception and continued reinterpretation from his own time until today. It will also defend the approach adopted throughout the present book, which takes Maimonides' arguments to be both sincere and philosophically serious. There is an important body of scholarship that argues for the contrary view, holding that many of the positions Maimonides adopts in the *Guide* are not meant to be taken at face value and that he never held to the theological opinions he explicitly espoused. Scholars debate whether he ought to be understood to believe in the opinions he presents as his own, which are the opinions that I try to explain in this book. Often, he is said to have secretly agreed with the opinions he claims to critique and reject. Among the evidence drawn on to argue the case, support is taken from claims about the *Guide*'s overall nature. Since the *Guide* is considered to be Maimonides' major philosophical work, and it will feature heavily in the rest of this book, it is appropriate here to introduce it, its purpose, and how it relates to the Jewish and philosophical streams on which it builds.

Some of the classic works of Rabbinic Judaism have been likened to a tree, with a trunk following a central line and branches shooting off in many different directions, addressing apparently unrelated or tangential issues. The *Guide* fits well into this tradition. Its structure is not immediately clear, to the degree that some even question whether there is an overarching design at all. For centuries, commentators and scholars have debated whether or not it follows the arrangements of other parts of Maimonides' work. Individual sections may also raise structural questions. What, for instance, is the relationship between the fourteen books of the *Code* and the fourteen categories into which Maimonides divides the commandments in the *Guide* (3:35, 535), assuming that there is such a relationship? The question is further complicated if one were also to try taking into account fourteen principles that Maimonides discusses that enable him to classify the commandments in an earlier work, the *Book of Commandments*, but, again, seem not to parallel the contents of the other lists of fourteen. Aside from its relationship to Maimonides' other works and his overall thought, the plan of the *Guide* itself is often obscure. In order to understand the work fully, Maimonides tells readers that they need to piece together information from separate chapters:

> If you wish to grasp the totality of what this Treatise contains, so that nothing of it will escape you, then you must connect its chapters one with another; and when reading a given chapter, your intention must be not only to understand the totality of the subject of that chapter, but also to grasp each word that occurs in it in the course of the speech, even if that word does not belong to the intention of the chapter.

The *Guide's* content also belongs to rabbinic literature. From the outset, Maimonides situates it in the tradition of Jewish exegesis. He states that 'the first purpose of this treatise is to explain the meanings of certain terms occurring in books of prophecy' (1: Introduction, 5). The task is necessary because many terms have diverse meanings and people are often misled when they do not take account of the various alternatives. They might conclude that the text teaches something false, and therefore end up 'perplexed' by the conflict between what they think true and what scripture teaches. There is a danger that such people either reject the text's authority altogether or, alternatively, abandon their reason and accept that the incorrect meaning is true. Maimonides continues:

> This Treatise also has a second purpose: namely, the explanation of very obscure parables occurring in the books of the prophets, but not explicitly identified there as such. Hence an ignorant or heedless individual might think that they possess only an external sense, but no internal one. However, even when one who truly possesses knowledge considers these parables and interprets them according to their external meaning, he too is overtaken by great perplexity. But if we explain these parables to him or if we draw his attention to their being parables, he will take the right road and be delivered from this perplexity. That is why I have called this Treatise 'The *Guide for the Perplexed*'.

In Maimonides' view, much of scripture possesses an 'external', surface meaning and an 'internal', deeper meaning. The deeper meaning is philosophical. In some cases, the external meaning is 'worth nothing' (1: Introduction, 11). In others, however, the surface meaning is also valuable. The book of *Proverbs* is an example, because its explicit teaching involves moral advice while

Maimonides takes its inner meaning to be teaching about scientific matters, chiefly the relationship between matter and form. Maimonides says that this relationship is even expressed in a verse from *Proverbs*, which reads 'A word fitly spoken is like apples of gold in settings of silver' (1: Introduction, 11). Of these parables, he writes that 'their external meaning contains wisdom that is useful in many respects, among which is the welfare of human societies, as is shown by the external meaning of Proverbs and of similar sayings. Their internal meaning, on the other hand, contains wisdom that is useful for beliefs concerned with the truth as it is' (1: Introduction, 12).[4] Maimonides wishes to draw attention to the parabolic nature of all of these passages, and either to explain the deeper meaning or present the reader with enough information to work it out alone.

The *Guide's* primary purpose is, then, exegesis and teaching, even though it is not an ordinary textbook arranged in such a way as to make it as easy as possible by explaining ideas in a clear, logical order. Instead, readers must piece together Maimonides' puzzles. Furthermore, how the chapters fit together or follow one from another is not the only problem they face. Philosophical arguments in the *Guide* can be difficult to make sense of. Many believe that they are intentionally incoherent. I do not. However, they are certainly presented in ways that often make them hard to follow, and at least some of the difficulty is intended: the *Guide* is an esoteric book, in the sense that it is aimed at a select group of people, not at everyone. Partly for this reason, the question of intentional incoherence lies at the heart of much of the secondary literature dealing with the *Guide's* esotericism. Such discussions are generated, at least to some degree, by Maimonides himself. At the end of the *Guide's* introduction, he explains seven different kinds of contradictories or contrary statements that occur in different literary works. He says that he will make use of two of them in the *Guide*. People disagree about whether they really are present and, if so, what their purpose is, but they are a major hermeneutical tool and are often invoked. A popular approach today holds that Maimonides intentionally contradicts himself in order to hide his real philosophical opinion about some theological questions. Since this issue is central to such a good deal of scholarship, I will say more about it in Chapter 7, together with discussing the different ways in which the *Guide* is understood and the ways in which it seems to be a book with a unique form. I will explain that there is no need to accept this view since the contradictions can be explained in a different way. I think that he uses the contradiction in order to keep secret some of his scriptural exegesis rather than to conceal his own theological or philosophical beliefs. The question of what Maimonides is doing when he employs this contradiction should be distinguished from the question about what he really thought about the theological problems he discusses. They are two separate issues. I believe that this distinction between the way in which Maimonides uses contradictions, on the one hand, and that of how he presents his 'true opinion', on the other, allows us to read the *Guide* as a more stimulating philosophical text than if it is an exercise in dissimulation. Maimonides was a significant thinker, not merely a follower of earlier philosophers, and our challenge in reading the *Guide* is not limited to hermeneutics but also to working through philosophical problems. I will therefore not be using the contradictions to uncover hidden theological beliefs. Nevertheless, it is important to mention them here because questions about the coherence of Maimonides' arguments will crop up in coming chapters.

One of the reasons that an author would write in an obscure fashion is to make sure that only those with the necessary training are able to understand the work. From the letter with which the *Guide* begins, it is clear that Maimonides needs to write in a certain way in order to ensure that it is pitched at the appropriate audience. He addresses it to a pupil, Joseph ben Judah, who had studied together with him but moved to Aleppo, and explains that 'your absence moved me to compose this Treatise, which I have composed for you and for those like you, however few they are' (1: Introduction, 4). The *Guide* is a work aimed at a special kind of reader and, therefore, a limited audience. What Maimonides teaches is not appropriate for everyone, but that presents him with a difficulty, for 'if someone explained all those matters in a book, he in effect would be teaching them to thousands of men' (1: Introduction, 7). Maimonides therefore has to find a way to communicate with such readers while avoiding teaching those whom he would not teach in person, and to do this, he needs to write a special kind of book. It is also important that the *Guide* was written in order to replace the way in which Maimonides was able to teach Joseph face to face. When teachers talk with someone in front of them, they can adapt what they say to the particular circumstances, taking into account the pupil's reactions, making sure only to reveal what will benefit the individual who is listening, and doing so in a way appropriate to that specific person. Books cannot be so tailor-made, but Maimonides' methods of presentation are aimed at reproducing this situation of individual tutorials as far as possible.

By presenting ideas in an unusual way and attempting to write with multiple audiences in mind, Maimonides could be seen to be imitating the Bible itself. He argues that the Bible uses parables and equivocal terms in order to communicate with various kinds of people. 'That which is said about all this is in equivocal terms so that the multitude might comprehend them in accord with the capacity of their understanding and the weakness of their representation, whereas the perfect man, who is already informed, will comprehend them otherwise' (1: Introduction, 9). Of course, the Bible is aimed at the entire community, not only an elite. Maimonides writes of his own book too that 'every beginner will derive benefit from some of the chapters of this Treatise, though he lacks even an inkling of what is involved in speculation' (1: Introduction, 16). Nevertheless, it is clear that the *Guide's* target audience is more limited, and he adds other strategies. Requiring students to work and piece together his exegesis from hints scattered around the book is one of them. Another is to write in a way that is intelligible only to more advanced readers. Even though Maimonides uses philosophy and the science of his day throughout, and you need to know a considerable amount of philosophy to understand the *Guide*, he states several times that he does not intend to explain the philosophical background in detail. The ideal reader will already be expert in many sciences and will be able to employ them in reading the *Guide*, but will also need to continue studying philosophical works and considering whether they are relevant to the points Maimonides makes. If something that Maimonides writes seems unintelligible or wrong, he asks readers to continue thinking about it. 'You therefore should not let your fantasies elaborate on what is said here, for that would hurt me and be of no use to yourself. You ought rather to learn everything that ought to be learned and constantly study this Treatise' (1: Introduction, 15). As well as demanding that readers pick up on hints to other parts of the *Guide* in order to understand it properly, Maimonides expects them to read widely and recognise allusions to other philosophical texts. Only those who are able to do so will benefit fully from the *Guide*.

Before diving into the substance of Maimonides' opinions, something should be said about his philosophical sources, since there are names that will appear repeatedly over the course of the coming chapters. For the sake of the issues explored here, the most important background is to be found in the Arabic Aristotelians. Along with other works of Greek science, Aristotle's books were translated into Arabic and creatively integrated into the philosophical curriculum. When Maimonides writes about Aristotle, it is Aristotle as mediated through this tradition. Philosophers who engaged in this project did not simply ape and preserve Aristotle, as is sometimes said, but developed his thought in new and exciting ways. A school of them flourished in Baghdad in the tenth century, the most prominent being al-Fārābī (c. 870–950/1), whose works Maimonides employed and rated extremely highly. Aristotle became known as 'the first teacher' and al-Fārābī as 'the second teacher', titles given by Avicenna (c. 970–1037), who was perhaps the most important of the Arabic philosophers. Avicenna reworked many of the ideas found in earlier philosophers and left an original body of thought. Maimonides mentions Avicenna by name only in a letter, not in any of his major works. Exactly what Maimonides knew of Avicenna's writing is debated, as is the question of whether he learned Avicenna's arguments from Avicenna's own works or from another source, but there is no doubt that Avicenna is crucial to understanding parts of the *Guide*. Averroes (1126–1198) was not satisfied with many of Avicenna's arguments and wished to return to what he considered a purer form of Aristotle's teachings. Whereas Avicenna created his own summae not explicitly built around Aristotle's texts, Averroes wrote, among many other things, commentaries on Aristotle, and became known in the Latin world as 'the Commentator'. Like Maimonides, he was born in Cordoba, and only shortly before Maimonides, but it is uncertain which of Averroes' works Maimonides read and when he would have come across them. Nevertheless, Averroes represents a crucial strand of Aristotelian philosophy and many have understood Maimonides through him.

Al-Fārābī, Avicenna and Averroes are the most famous among the group known as 'the philosophers'. They are often contrasted with the Mutakallimūn, or kalām, who are labelled 'the theologians' and are themselves divided into several different movements. Maimonides generally objected to their scientific theories and sometimes used them as a foil when explaining his own views. It is also worth mentioning al-Ghazālī (c. 1056–1111) in this context, as one of the most important thinkers of the time, although his name does not appear much in the present book. Al-Ghazālī has often been considered an adherent of kalām theology and an opponent of the philosophers. Today, scholars believe that he was far more complex, and integrated much of the philosophers' thought while still maintaining some independence from them. It is difficult to categorise him as belonging exclusively to either the philosophers or the theologians; he sometimes seems to inhabit a place in between. Comparisons between al-Ghazālī and Maimonides have been made with increasing frequency in recent decades, and a number of scholars have sought evidence that Maimonides was influenced by al-Ghazālī. Presumably, Maimonides' own objections to the philosophers are partly responsible for the apparent affinity between him and al-Ghazālī, although Maimonides' critiques seem more limited, even if they have parallels in al-Ghazālī. Whether or not the criticisms are fair is less important for our purposes than the arguments that Maimonides makes in response.

Perhaps it will be surprising that I have not yet named any Jewish philosophers. Among those who preceded Maimonides, there were indeed major Jewish philosophers writing in Arabic. Some have suggested that he may have been influenced in particular details by Saadya Gaon, Abraham Ibn Ezra, or Judah Halevi, for example, but their impact is not so obvious and they seem not to have left a great impression on those of Maimonides' arguments that are considered in this book. In any case, when assessing philosophical claims, the religious affiliations of those advancing the arguments is less important to Maimonides than the arguments themselves. One of his most famous lines reads 'hear the truth from whoever says it' (*Eight Chapters*, 60). It echoes a common sentiment among Arabic thinkers, that an argument should be judged on its own merits, independently of its origin or its proponent's status. The best way to establish a claim's veracity is to consider the reasons for or against it, not the identity of those who believe it. The same is true of reading the *Guide*. Many works written today claim to present Maimonides' real opinion on philosophical and theological matters and the rhetoric used in support of different interpretations can sometimes be very strong. Ultimately, readers need to weigh up the various explanations given to Maimonides' thought and that can only be done by studying the *Guide*. I hope that this book will help to do exactly that and also contribute to the ongoing debates about how to interpret Maimonides.

2

Life and Humanity

The most convenient place to begin reading about how Maimonides understands what it means to be human is in the earliest of his major works, his commentary on the Mishnah, which is a running commentary that also contains some longer, more elaborate sections. These include an introduction to the entire Mishnah as well as introductions to other sections that count as standalone pieces in their own right. One of them became known as *Eight Chapters*, and serves as the introduction to a part called *Sayings of the Fathers*. *Sayings* is an unusual piece of the Mishnah since, unlike other Mishnaic tractates, its main focus is not legal. Instead, it consists of a collection of sayings and proverbs attributed to various sages. Nevertheless, it is situated towards the end of a part of the Mishnah that deals with damages and legal disagreements. Maimonides says that such a position is appropriate because *Sayings* is crucial for the judges who rule on the basis of these Mishnaic discussions. The reason is that in *Sayings*, the sages teach behaviour required in order to form positive character traits and judges are those most in need of virtuous character. Judges need to be in control when in session so as not to reveal things to witnesses. A judge also needs to be in control outside of the courtroom, so as to be respected by the public who must abide by adjudications. Moreover, it is particularly important for people with such positions to possess good character, as a vicious judge would harm not only herself. Vicious judges harm others too. A judge needs to be temperate, of steadfast character, and to be resolute, otherwise her rulings could be influenced by extraneous and tangential factors. *Sayings of the Fathers* is therefore a crucial aspect of the Mishnah's judicial parts.

Although *Sayings* is appropriately situated because of its relevance to those passing judgement, Maimonides explains that it is important for everyone, since good character is necessary for humans to flourish. Accordingly, *Sayings* teaches not only about character traits, but virtues generally, and that includes the intellectual virtues. At one point in the commentary, Maimonides states that the goal of the tractate is to 'provide education for a person to aid in the endeavour to improve his soul through virtues of character traits and reason'. As it is an introduction to the tractate, *Eight Chapters* therefore explains how humans must behave in order to perfect their souls. To understand Maimonides' view of *Sayings of the Fathers* adequately, then, one must understand what he means by soul generally, and by the human soul in particular which, as will become clear, is equivalent to understanding what it is to be a human. Since Maimonides outlines the soul only very concisely, in the first of the *Eight Chapters*, it will be helpful to elaborate on what his view entails. In doing so, I will sometimes depart from Maimonides' own texts in order to explain some background ideas that I think are helpful.

Maimonides adopts a standard Aristotelian account of the soul. It is one that might seem surprising to many today. There is a widespread tendency among the general population to think that souls and bodies are two separate things that are combined into a person, and that, if there really is any such thing as a soul, body and soul both continue to exist in their different ways after the person has ceased to be. Sometimes a soul is then considered to be the true essence of a person, while the body is merely a vessel containing it, which it uses in order to function in the material world. This is not what Maimonides means by soul. In his view, as for Aristotle, both bodies and souls are components of a human, but neither exists as particularly human bodies or souls independently of one another. Neither a human soul nor a human body is enough to make up a person. Humans have bodies but are not their bodies. I am different from this particular piece of matter that is my body. I was me several years ago when my body was different and even made up of different atoms. Moreover, were I to die, what is now my body would no longer be me. It would not be a human being at all, but a corpse. As a human being is a psycho-physical entity, it is also true of my soul that it would not be me if it is divested of body. A soul is a component of a thing that is alive but a soul does not exist without a body.

While it is true to say that Maimonides considered the soul to be in some sense equivalent to the 'essence', what is meant is not that the soul is more authentically human than a human body, but that the soul accounts for what kind of thing a person is; 'soul is the "form" of a natural body that is potentially alive'.[1] A distinction between 'form' and 'body', or 'form' and 'matter', explains how there can be different things of the same kind. We can distinguish objects as different things either by describing their different features or by locating them in different physical spaces. There are oak trees and panthers, and we can explain that they are different kinds of things because of the differences in their natures and in the ways they behave. One is a kind of vegetation and the other is a kind of feline. The differences between two separate oak trees cannot be explained in this way. Of course, two oaks might have different accidental features, like size or age, but they cannot be distinguished by different natures, as they both possess the nature of an oak tree. Instead, they are differentiated by being separate material substances. A substance is something that exists in its own right, not as part of something else, so a tree is a substance, while its colour is an accident that exists in it. The idea that a substance's form tells you what the thing is can be expressed by saying that the form is what accounts for its nature, so is shared by objects of a single species, while the matter of these things is their individuating principle. There is an analogy in how a piece of wood can be divided up and made into a table and a chair. What the objects are does not depend on the piece of wood they are made out of but on the form that the carpenter imposes on them. Form is what makes something what it is. In the case of two chairs with identical forms, they are distinguished by being in different bits of matter. However, if all you know is that the object is made out of wood, that doesn't give you information about what it is, whether it is a table or a chair. You know what the object is by knowing what form it has.

It may seem that knowing the form is not enough, however, because we are said to know something when we know all of its causes, and Aristotle divides causes into four kinds. Matter and form are the material and formal causes, and objects also have final and efficient causes. It is clear that knowing something must include knowing at least the formal cause, since the formal cause is an object's nature, its form. A final cause is the object's aim or purpose, so the chair's final cause is to be sat on. In certain cases, formal and final causes can be identified with one another: in order to see what something is, you look at its characteristic behaviour, what it tends to do. Consider a seed, for example, which has the formal cause of a tree. Given the right conditions, the seed automatically grows into the tree. The formal cause is in the seed potentially and in the tree actually, as the tree results from a process of the form's actualisation. A seed has a natural tendency to grow into a tree, to actualise its form. This is what the object aims at, and is its final cause or its purpose. It is also what is good for the object, because everything aims at its own good and its actualisation, so Aristotle writes that 'the good has rightly been declared to be that at which all things aim'.[2] Since the final cause expresses the tendency that the nature imbues, which is the object's goal and what is good for it, the formal and final causes of the potential tree can be identified with one another. The efficient cause is also the same as the formal cause, since 'like causes like', which is to say that something causes something else of the same kind to come to be. This is most obvious in natural generation: A horse gives birth to a foal and an owl to an owlet. Offspring share the nature of their parents, their formal cause. The formal and final causes, the nature and its purpose, are therefore shared by the object and its efficient cause. To know an animal properly is to know these causes. Knowing them would also grant a kind of understanding of the material cause, since the knowledge would include knowing what sort of matter a certain object is made out of, like bone or bark. To know something's causes is therefore to know its nature.

As the form of a living body, soul is a particular kind of form. A soul is considered a principle of life, so anything that is alive in any way has a soul. For the Aristotelians, investigating the soul is the same as investigating what it means to say that something is alive, that it is animate. On their view, every animal is said to have a soul, since all animals are animate. Plants are also alive, so plants have souls too. To be alive is to be a self-mover, with the capacity to grow and reproduce. Living things therefore have an internal principle of motion. Such a principle distinguishes them from inanimate objects, which do not move themselves but, instead, are moved by something external. It is true that things like stones move downwards of their own accord, if they are not prevented from doing so, whereas fire and heat move upwards. They do so, however, not owing to an internal principle of motion but, rather, because they have a natural tendency towards a particular position. Once they are in those positions, they rest rather than move. Aristotle explained this phenomenon by conceiving of separate elements that, together, constitute physical beings. He called them earth, water, air and fire on the basis of their relative mixtures of the properties signified by hot, cold, dry and moist. Everything in our world can be conceived as a blend of these properties. Objects that are predominantly made up of solid or liquid, earth or water, will naturally move towards the centre, whereas those that are made up mostly of air or fire move away from the centre. Without outside interference, inanimate objects naturally tend towards their resting places. Once a stone has reached its natural position, resting on the earth, it will not move by itself but only if propelled by an external force. It was therefore said that natural motion has only one direction: down, towards the centre, in the case of heavy bodies, and up, away from the centre, in the case of light bodies. Natural motion is rectilinear; it is motion in a single direction and, provided there are no external impulses, it is also straight, because an inanimate body intrinsically moves directly towards its natural location. By contrast, living things move in multiple ways and are caused to do so by an internal principle.

For the Aristotelians, then, to say that something is alive is to say that it is a natural unit possessing its own principle of motion; unlike an inanimate object, it is a self-mover. This much is true of all living things, both plants and animals. But, of course, although all living things move themselves, so carrots and cockroaches are both said to be ensouled, the ways in which they do so are different. What is common to all of them is that they respond in particular ways to specific environmental stimuli. Active reaction of some sort is therefore a crucial difference between animals and inanimate things. An external stimulant prompts a tendency in the animal to react in certain ways, depending on the kinds of faculties the animal possesses. As the form accounts for what something is, the individual's soul is what determines how it responds; so, for example, sunlight causes a different reaction in a plant from that which it causes in a cat. The plant would photosynthesise, while the cat might merely bask and warm itself. Light causes a different reaction in the two organisms because they have different faculties. Both have faculties of a vegetative kind, but they feed themselves in different ways. Maimonides explains that a human's nutritive part, for example, is not the same as the nutritive part belonging to a donkey or a horse. 'For a human is nourished by the nutritive part of the human soul, a donkey is nourished by the nutritive part of the donkey's soul, and a palm tree is nourished by the nutritive part of its soul. Now, all these individuals are said to be "nourished" solely due to the equivocal character of the word, not because the meaning itself is one' (*Eight Chapters*, 62). The vegetative faculties in the donkey use different organs from those in the palm tree, and work in a manner closer to those of other animals than to those of plants, even though the souls of diverse kinds of animals are as different from one another as the animals themselves are different.

Animals all share further abilities that plants do not. They are sensitive and responsive in more ways. While plants and animals both respond to light and heat, an animal behaves differently if you shine a light on its back from how it behaves if you shine the light in its eyes. An animal has extra faculties for which it has extra organs. Maimonides calls these faculties 'sentient', 'imaginative' and 'appetitive'. The sentient part is so termed because it 'consists of the five powers well known to the multitude: sight, hearing, taste, smell and touch'. Through these senses we perceive and understand the external world, and they are used by the other faculties as well. When we represent something to ourselves in the imagination, for example, we use images that we first acquire through sense experience. The imagination retains these physical impressions and also has the ability to combine them in novel ways that do not correspond to anything existing in external reality, outside of the mind or imagination, so you can imagine an elephant with wings or other such fantastical creatures and events, even though you may never have seen them. 'From things it has perceived, this power puts together things it has not perceived at all and which are not possible for it to perceive. For example, a man imagines an iron ship floating in the air, or an individual whose head is in the heavens and whose feet are on the earth, or an animal with a thousand eyes. The imaginative power puts together many such impossible things and makes them exist in the imagination.' Maimonides describes the 'appetitive' part as 'the power by which a man desires, or is repulsed by, a certain thing'. It causes animals to seek what they need, and what is agreeable to them, and to flee from things that harm them. It is also the seat of emotions like fear and rage, which motivate the animal to carry out these actions. This part makes use of an animal's organs. In order for an animal to satisfy its desires, it employs 'the power of the hand for hitting, the power of the foot for walking, the power of the eye for seeing, and the power of the heart for being bold or fearful. Likewise, the rest of the organs – both internal and external – and their powers are instruments for this appetitive power.'

Soul itself is indivisible, even though philosophers refer to its different parts. 'By saying "parts" they do not mean that the soul is divided into parts as bodies are divided into parts. Indeed, they regard the different actions of the totality of the soul as parts of a whole composed of those parts' (*Eight Chapters*, 61). We differentiate the parts on the basis of the single soul's various activities, not because they are separate things. Cutting up an animal would not create two parts with separate souls, or separate bits of soul. It would create two bodies, one of which is ensouled, if the animal remains alive, and the other not. Organs are characteristic of living beings, and are used by the soul to carry out those functions that require precisely such organs. Seeing requires an eye, hearing an ear, speaking a tongue, and so on. If they are physical, the organs can be separated from their host, but they would no longer be organs that the soul uses in order to act. A crocodile's leg is an organ that it uses to move around. If you remove it from the crocodile, it is no longer a leg at all, but an inanimate piece of matter, albeit one with the shape of a crocodile leg. It would be quite safe to approach a dismembered leg but it would not be wise if the leg is still attached to the crocodile. To be a leg is to be a part of the entire animal and to carry out a function that is part of the animal's behaviour. As an organ, the leg bears a particular relationship to the organism. Living creatures are prior to the organs they grow. An organ is something that is not an independent object in its own right but, rather, functions by being part of the particular living whole. Machines, on the other hand, are posterior to their parts as their forms are imposed by artifice on pre-existing components. This is why a watch can be dismantled and then reassembled but a flower cannot. Taking the parts of a watch and putting them together would generate a perfectly good watch, but putting the parts of a flower together would not make the result a real, living flower. Instead, the flower grows from what is already potentially a flower. The flower's form pre-exists.

Living things are distinguished from inanimate ones by being autonomous movers. By calling them natural units, we distinguish them from artificial units as well. The parts of an animal are organically united, so that something that causes a reaction in an animal's sense organ causes a reaction that makes a difference to the animal as a whole. The organ's activity is relevant to the entire body, which means that an amputated leg is no longer a leg, since it no longer has the relevant function. And when we consider an animal's action, we say that it is the animal that acts, not only the organ with which it does so. For example, we say that a lion roars with its mouth but we wouldn't say that the mouth itself roars independently, or we say that I feel pain in my arm rather than that my arm feels pain. The form is what constitutes the animal, and the parts are, in a sense, posterior. They take their meanings and function from the animal as a whole. Natural things have an essence that explains what they are. This is true of animals but not machines. Machines are not living beings, and neither are they natural units. Artificial things are put together by an external maker and their parts could be replaced with no real alteration to the artefact itself.

It should now be clear that, because a soul is a kind of natural form, Maimonides means to distinguish living beings from those things that do not move of their own accord, which include artificial objects, even those that apparently move themselves, like robots or cars. It should also be clear that there are different kinds of souls. Animals react to stimuli in a particular way, depending on the sort of faculties they have, and their reactions differ depending on what kind of animal they are. One way to emphasise the variety of incommensurable experiences had by different kinds of animals is to consider the 'estimative' faculty. Maimonides mentions it in the *Guide* (1:46, 102), and it is an idea advanced by Avicenna and other medieval philosophers to account for the phenomenon of recognising something that is not perceptible. The estimative faculty is able to perceive something that is not presented to any one of the external faculties, but is derived from the entirety of the sense perceptions together and goes beyond them to conclude something more. Through this faculty, for example, a sheep can sense a wolf's hostility. However, the faculty differs in different animals, and they would react very differently to one another. The sheep would experience fear, while the wolf would be more likely to begin salivating. Even if their souls have similar functions, the faculties are not exactly identical, which illustrates that different kinds of animals are conditioned by their features to behave in different ways and to experience the world differently. It is not simply that they have different perceptual equipment but that they are entirely different beings with entirely different souls. We could say 'dangerous' exists in the wolf physically, in that it is dangerous, and in the sheep experientially, in that it senses that the wolf is dangerous. Estimation enables animals to piece together information to tell them something about the world and, in this limited sense, it could be considered a very basic form of reason. However, as truly rational beings, humans are different again because they can also come to an understanding of what this means. We can have thoughts about the meaning of 'menace', not only passively experience danger.

I mentioned above that Maimonides considers the subject of *Sayings of the Fathers* to be the human good, so his focus in *Eight Chapters* is on the human soul and its faculties. A human being possesses the same functions as other living beings, as well as intellect, but Maimonides explains that the human soul is not actually divisible into its separate parts. Instead, the soul is one, but it has a variety of operations. Many of them have analogues in activities of other animals. There is nevertheless a crucial difference. While other animals carry out their activities naturally – spiders spin webs; birds build nests – the characteristically human activity is carried out only after deliberation over a course of action or after studying the sciences. To be sure, humans also have faculties that behave in ways similar to those of other animals. Humans belong to a biological species and are naturally necessitated to operate in certain ways, such as growing, digesting, regulating our own body temperatures, and myriad other such processes. As explained above, these functions are all part of what is termed the 'vegetative' or 'nutritive' part of the soul, the part that is responsible for nourishment, growth, and reproduction, and these are operations that all living things possess. However, humans do these things as a result of their specifically human souls, so the way in which humans feed differs from ways in which flies or flowers do. 'Certain actions necessarily stem from one soul and other actions from another soul. One action may resemble another action, so that the two actions are thought to be identical even though they are not.' This is because the function is part of the life of the entire organism, and the organism lives a different sort of life from that of other kinds of animals. There are similarities, of course, but Maimonides states that they must nonetheless be thought to be products of different souls. Moreover, although a human soul has similarities with souls of other animals, it differs from them in a way that sets it apart qualitatively from other animals. Humans are particular kinds of animals, animals that are rational.

The difference between humans and other animals is, in Maimonides' view, not quite the same as the differences between dogs and cats, or horses and hens. All animate beings are part of a species and, as such, the individuals transcend themselves, because they are part of a larger group and because they reproduce. Like other animals, humans belong to a species that transcends each individual human. However, humans reach beyond their individual limitations in a different way as well. I will consider this more in Chapter 3, when addressing what Maimonides has to say about divine providence. For now, however, it is important to note that what it is to be a member of the human species is to have a human soul, a soul with faculties that are unlike those of other animals. Aristotelians therefore argued that humans can function in ways that have no analogous activities in other animals, which is why the Aristotelian definition of a human is 'rational animal'. In the Aristotelian system, definitions consist of two parts, a genus and a differentia, which, together, compare and differentiate. Through a genus, something is likened to other objects with which it shares certain essential features. The differentia, or specific difference, sets it apart from objects of different species belonging to the same genus. A human's definition, rational animal, includes the genus 'animal', comparing it to other animals, and the specific difference 'reason', which distinguishes the human species from others, like sheep or felines. To understand what a human is, in the Aristotelian view, you therefore need to understand what it is to be an animal generally and, also, what it is to be rational, which is done by considering the ways in which rational activity expresses itself.

Rational activity is varied, so Maimonides explains that 'the rational part is the power found in man by which he perceives intelligibles, deliberates, acquires the sciences, and distinguishes between base and noble actions'. Since 'some of these activities are practical and some are theoretical', the intellect is divided into practical and theoretical (also known as speculative) parts. The practical can be subdivided into its 'productive' and 'reflective' functions. 'The productive is the power by means of which we acquire occupations, such as carpentry, agriculture, medicine, and navigation.' Such activities are necessary for a human life and are acquired through study. 'The reflective is that by which one deliberates about a thing he wishes to do at the time he wishes to do it – whether it is possible to do it or not and, if it is possible, how it ought to be done.' A capacity to reflect requires the ability to envisage an aim that you want to achieve and to think about the best way to arrive there. It is possible for humans to respond to a question about why they did something by giving a reason other than biological necessity. Ethical considerations also belong to this capacity. Ethics is one of the main topics of *Eight Chapters*, and I will touch on it below. The practical intellect's activities are required both to enable people to perfect their individual humanity and for them to live together in a community. Society living is, in Maimonides' view, necessary in order for humans to reach their perfection. Unlike birds, who seem to learn with relative ease how to build their nests and carry out the various activities that enable them to live and reproduce, humans need much more in order simply to exist, so there are far more activities they perform that are characteristically human and aimed at living a human life. In the introduction to the Mishnah commentary, Maimonides explains that in order to be self-sufficient, someone would need to learn how to farm, to cook, to make clothes, to build, and to fashion tools for all of these activities. 'And the life of Methuselah is not long enough to study all of these crafts that someone needs in order to live. And when would one find free time to study and to acquire wisdom?'

Because their specific difference is reason, humans carry out the activities that enable them to be part of the particularly human species after study and reflection. However, to be part of the human species by living together and creating a society is only partially to engage in being fully human. Being social requires activities that stem from the practical part of the rational soul but not the theoretical part. The practical intellect deals with those activities that are directed to a purpose other than their own activity, and they result in actions, the theoretical intellect's activity is not directed towards something external. It is an end in itself. Maimonides states that 'by means of the theoretical, man knows the essence of the unchanging beings'. This could be taken in two ways, although they do not necessarily have to conflict with each other. One interpretation is that Maimonides is talking about knowing the essences of immaterial substances that exist separate from matter and, therefore, do not change. The other is that he is talking about knowing unchanging essences of changing things. I mentioned above that the distinction between matter and form helps to explain how there can be different things of the same kind. It also explains how things can change. Aristotle distinguished between different kinds of change. He argued that change requires three elements: the changing thing, the feature that it lacks, the feature that it acquires.[3] The nature of the object that changes is constant. When a tree grows leaves, for example, the tree has a new feature because something that was lacking, but was potentially part of the tree, is now actual. However, although the tree has changed, it remains a tree, so it continues to possess the same nature. Instead, what has changed is one of the tree's accidents, a feature that can change without the substance itself being annihilated. The other kind of change is substantial change. This would take place if the tree were to become something else, if the tree were to die, as a result of which it would no longer possess the same nature. The object that was a tree would

then be a different kind of thing, inanimate wood. The tree's form
no longer exists. However, what has ceased to be is not the form
generally, which continues to exist in other trees of the same kind,
but the form of this particular tree. So even though the nature of
this particular wooden object has changed, the abstract nature of a
tree, what it is to be an oak, for instance, has not. The form persists
and is not affected by substantial or accidental changes occurring to
individuals. Recall that to know something is to know its essence,
what I described at the beginning of this chapter as its formal
cause. Since the abstract form of a tree itself does not change, as
a particular change happens to an individual tree rather than to
trees generally, contemplating the form involves contemplating
something unchanging. These unchanging forms belong to all
natural beings, and they are the objects of theoretical reason.

In order to be the best possible human, Maimonides argues
that theoretical reason must be perfected, as it is a particularly
human characteristic. Perfecting the intellect depends on perfecting
character traits, since balanced character leads to the possibility
of intellectual perfection. So Maimonides will continue to insist
that virtuous character is critical but, rather than the goal itself,
it is a prerequisite that enables intellectual perfection. The rest of
Eight Chapters deals mostly with training character traits and with
morality, but there is more detail about what Maimonides means
by theoretical reason, and its ramifications, in the *Guide for the
Perplexed*. One of the major topics the *Guide* deals with is human
nature and felicity, which is considered both at its beginning and its
end. The opening two chapters revisit the topic of the true human
'form' in the context of explaining the story of Eden in Genesis.
Here, Maimonides writes that the 'image of God' in which humans
are said to be fashioned in Genesis 1:26, when God says 'let us make
Adam in our image after our likeness', is the intellect. Many people
believed that it refers to a physical form, and thought that the bible
teaches that God has a humanlike body. Maimonides insists that
this is a mistake and that 'image' in this context does not refer to
an object's physical shape. Instead, he explains, 'image' is used to
mean the Aristotelian form, and the 'image of God' is an aspect of
the human form that distinguishes people from other animals, i.e.,
intellect. To recap briefly, substantial forms are how we distinguish
different objects. Together with the matter of a particular object, the
form constitutes an individual substance. Above, I explained that
while a material object has body, body alone is not what that object
is. It is rather a body of a particular kind. What sort of body it is

depends on the form, and the form is captured through a definition, which includes a specific difference marking out the species to which the object belongs. Since the human species is differentiated from all other animals by reason, reason is that part of the human form that Genesis calls the 'divine image', says Maimonides. He then goes even further and limits the divine image to the speculative intellect, which contemplates truth, rather than the practical intellect, which deals with good and bad.

The *Guide's* final four chapters, which Maimonides describes as a unit forming 'a kind of conclusion', include a good deal about human perfection and the proper worship of God, which is intellectual. The context of the section I cite here is divine providence and, in particular, the providence that extends to virtuous and perfect people. Again, Maimonides explains his insights as part of an exegetical treatment of certain biblical verses. One of them is Ps. 91:14: 'Because he has set his passionate love upon me, therefore I will deliver him; I will set him on high, because he has known my name.' In explaining why the verse uses a particular term to denote love of God, Maimonides describes a passionate love that results from grasping the intelligibles: 'You know the difference between the terms *"one who loves"* and *"one who loves passionately"*; an excess of love, so that no thought remains that is directed toward a thing other than the beloved, is passionate love' (3:51, 627). The *Code* also includes an expression of this kind of love: 'What is the love of God that is befitting? It is to love the Eternal with a great and exceeding love, so strong that one's soul shall be knit up with the love of God, and one should be continually enraptured by it, like a lovesick individual, whose mind is at no time free from his passion for a particular woman, the thought of her filling his heart at all times, when sitting down or rising up, when he is eating or drinking. Even more intense should be the love of God in the hearts of those who love him' (*Mishneh Torah*, 84).

By mentioning passionate love, both of these passages, but especially that in the *Code*, can give the impression that Maimonides is advocating for an emotional sort of worship. It is an impression that can be confusing, because we often connect emotions with sensual pleasure. Love for an object of affection like the love that Maimonides describes in the *Code* is not generally limited to intellectual contemplation. A passionate, obsessive love is focused on a particular person or thing, and if someone's thoughts are taken up with that thing, those thoughts include aspects that are particular to the object of love and, therefore, depend on the object's materiality. However, the passage in the *Guide* proceeds to explain that the passions and senses stand in the way of this intellectual love because they depend on the body. As is often the case, we need to bear in mind that Maimonides is here using a metaphor. In fact, he is talking about a love that is not sensual at all. The point he is making is that by its very nature, this kind of all-consuming love is available only to the intellect among the human faculties. Only the intellect can become so wrapped up in its object of perception that none of it remains unmoved, neither of the faculty nor the organ. This is why Maimonides says that intellectual worship is perception in which no room is left for anything other than the object of worship. To explain why this is so, it will be helpful to touch on human perception generally, and intellectual perception in particular. My purpose in doing so is not to explain fully how Maimonides understood perception, but simply to give some background to show that the intellectual faculty is the only human faculty capable of this kind of passionate love.

The most obvious form of perception is sense perception. Each of the five senses is limited to perceiving particular features, and the kind of perception is determined by its organ's material, so perception depends on the way that the perceiver is able to apprehend. Since a sense perceives exactly what is appropriate to its organ, it has certain ways in which it perceives its object. For example, sight perceives colour and smell perceives scent. The way to check whether something is rough or smooth is by feeling it, so touch reveals features appropriate to the organ it uses, in this case the skin. You wouldn't check what colour it is or how it smells by feeling it. When writing about intellectual perception, Maimonides states that it involves 'the union of cognition with what is cognised, which is, as it were, similar to the proximity of one body to another' (1:18, 43). It nonetheless differs from sense perception as its organ is immaterial. It stands to reason that the intellect is immaterial because its object is immaterial. Intellect perceives unchanging forms, rather than the material particulars apprehended by the senses, because it grasps what it is to be those things and can define them. The intellect is able to abstract essential features of any particular thing and understand what the thing is. For example, it can understand that a line is the shortest distance between two points even if a line in external reality exists only as the edge of a surface.

If the intellect is able to abstract from matter in such a way, it must itself be immaterial. However, this raises a difficulty about the relationship between the intellect and its object. In the case of sense experience, there is an obvious way in which a sense organ and its object are related. Take touch, for example, in which you feel an object that is related to the organ by being in an adjacent place. By contrast, since Maimonides claims that the intellect is immaterial, it is less obvious how there can be a connection between intellect and the concrete objects outside the mind. Aristotle explained that when you think about a stone, there is something about the stone in your mind but what is in your mind is obviously not the stone itself.[4] Instead, what is grasped is something about the object that is abstracted from matter. As explained above, the theoretical intellect has the intelligibles as its object of perception. These are the forms. Forms can exist in different ways. In one way, the form is the formal cause of a material being and, as such, it is the form of an individual and it exists in reality outside the mind, in the concrete thing. However, they can also exist devoid of matter in the mind. When they do so, they exist as universals. A form that exists in the mind is a universal because it can be predicated of many different individuals. When I think of a labrador's form, I can say that it belongs to all labradors and not only to a single individual. Nevertheless, even though Maimonides states that 'no species exists outside the mind' (3:18, 474), the form in the mind must bear some relationship to the physical labrador. The idea is that the intellect operates on images drawn from the senses and stored in the imagination. It abstracts from these images to form a conception of a labrador in the same way as it is able to abstract from physical representations of lines to an understanding about what a line is. Therefore, what exists in the intellect is precisely that which is appropriate to intellectual perception, just as what exists in a particular sense is what is appropriate to that sense's organ.

Returning to Maimonides' comment on Ps. 91:14, explaining what it means to say that someone '*loves passionately*', it is now possible to see that intellectual love is that which leaves no room for anything other than its object. When you touch something, the object remains distinct from the impression gained in the senses. By contrast, in the case of intellectual perception, the form understood is not material, so there is no such distinction between the intellect and its object. The intellect's activity is complete inasmuch as it is not hampered by a material organ. Unlike sensual perception, true intellectual perception involves subject and object becoming completely bound up with one another. In sum, although Maimonides explains intellectual perfection and worship in terms that sound mysteriously ecstatic to many readers, it is not necessary to read him as if he is advocating anything other than fulfilling the natural intellectual goal. There is an epistemological theory behind his explanation, and a general understanding of how perception works, which sets Maimonides' comments in line with his understanding of the intellect's natural powers. While someone engaged in this sort of intellectual contemplation would undoubtedly be experiencing, Maimonides is not advocating a kind of experience that is supra-rational and affords a kind of knowledge transcending the natural powers of human reason.[5] He is describing a situation in which the intellect is fully actualised and not distracted in any way by other parts of the soul.

There is nevertheless something to say for the claim that such intellectual perfection involves the ultimate form of pleasure available, even if Maimonides does not advocate anything other than fulfilling natural human capacities. Aristotle explains that we take pleasure in the activity of our senses when they are actively engaged in perceiving those things appropriate to them.[6] However, since they are material, they cannot take as strong a pleasure in their object of perception as the intellect can. All the other human faculties depend on a physical substrate that interferes with and limits the way in which the object of sensation is felt. A sense is capable of perceiving opposites, like hot or cold, so it must itself be between the two. The sense organ can be affected by either extreme. Moving from one extreme towards the contrary is pleasurable as it alleviates the pain that the material organ feels. However, were the organ placed in a permanently extreme state, it would be damaged and distorted. Similarly, the pleasures of one faculty can impede the pleasures of another. We find change pleasurable, says Aristotle, because our desires compete with one another.[7] Since we are complex beings, we need to satisfy different aspects, and when we are acting in a way that is pleasurable to one aspect we might be neglecting another. For example, when we eat we are satisfying a desire motivated by hunger but, in doing so, we might begin to feel thirsty so desire to drink instead. This is not true of the intellect. Intellectual pleasure lacks an opposite pain that it is trying to alleviate. It therefore has no excess and cannot become intemperate. Ultimately, because only in intellectual perception is the object of thought completely embraced by the faculty that grasps it, intellectual apprehension was considered the most pleasurable activity of all.

For the same reason that intellectual pleasure is the greatest form of pleasure, it is also the most permanent and the most intense.

Nevertheless, as people have souls that are dependent on bodies, Maimonides explains that they need to take time to rest too. 'For the soul becomes weary and the mind dull by continuous reflection upon difficult matters, just as the body becomes exhausted from undertaking toilsome occupations until it relaxes and rests and then returns to equilibrium' (*Eight Chapters*, 77). Material faculties tire, so the pleasures they experience cannot last. In chapter 5 of *Sayings*, there is a passage that reads as follows: 'any love that is dependent on something, when that thing perishes, the love perishes. But a love that is not dependent on something, does not ever perish.' Maimonides explains that a love dependent on something is a love for a physical object; the love disappears along with its object's demise. If the cause of love is 'something divine, i.e., true knowledge, that love cannot be removed ever, since its cause always exists'. As the body grows weaker and its need and desire for physical satisfaction diminishes, Maimonides explains, the intellect's ability to take pleasure in its proper object increases. Without the distractions presented by other human faculties, the intellect is strengthened (3:51, 627).

Human perfection involves intellectual perfection, in the form of theoretical contemplation, and intellectual perfection is worship of God. Maimonides identifies it with eternal life. Whereas some traditional religious thinkers are concerned to preserve what they consider to be a personal afterlife, Maimonides' view is that those parts of a human that physically distinguish her from other humans are the very same things that prevent her from experiencing this most intense form of pleasure. Without them, there is no way to distinguish individuals in the afterlife and Maimonides states that all souls that continue to exist 'are one in number' (1:74, 221). It therefore makes no sense to ask after the individual existence of John, as those characteristics that distinguish John from Miriam are not the features of humans that could in any way be said to survive John's demise. Instead, when somebody contemplates abstract truth, a part of them is bound up with that truth and, since truth does not perish along with the body, that part can be said to survive material passing.[8] At this point, some identify a basic tension in Maimonides' view of human perfection. On the one hand, the kind of perfection that humans can achieve seems to be for an individual alone. However, Maimonides is committed also to saying that a perfect person acts in particular ways towards others and not only to herself. Achieving human perfection involves ethical behaviour and Maimonides will have to consider how ethics and law contribute.

Until now, this chapter has been concerned with explaining what human nature is and, by extension, what the human goal is, not with how to get there. The specific human good was seen to be intellectual, but Maimonides claims that this perfection does not appear alone but only if bodily needs are satisfied and moral virtues acquired. Without these preliminary conditions, people would be too easily distracted and unable to engage in intellectual pursuits. The intellectual virtues are achieved only after a long process of training, although Maimonides admits that there may be very rare cases in which little or none is needed, and people are generally influenced by several factors that prevent them reaching the goal. Among them are natural dispositions and the habits they grew up with. He writes that a person's character 'is influenced by his neighbours and friends and follows the custom of the people in his country' (*Character Traits*, 46). Issues connected with these ethical questions take up much of the rest of *Eight Chapters*. Maimonides' overriding concern is to show how the law supports an Aristotelian virtue ethics. *Eight Chapters* is concerned with explaining that a good life involves inculcating moral virtue. Maimonides therefore explains what he considers virtue and vice to be. They are states of the soul, so he divides them into moral and rational, depending on which part of the soul they pertain to. Moral virtues 'are found only in the appetitive part, and the sentient part is in this case a servant of the appetitive part' (*Eight Chapters*, 65). They are at the mean between extremes, such as between lustfulness and insensitivity, or between cowardice and foolhardiness. The law helps people to attain this balance: prohibitions and commandments are put in place so 'that we move away from one side as a means of discipline' (*Eight Chapters*, 71). When people lean towards one of the extremes, they are vicious. Rational virtues such as wisdom and intelligence are not means since, as explained above, the intellect cannot become excessive and intemperate. The most rationally virtuous is someone who has a perfected intellect. The halakha aims at both of these, but it includes far more commandments designed to lead to moral virtue than to intellectual virtue, and moral virtue is the main focus of *Eight Chapters*.

Aristotle's ethics is not itself a set of rules, so the Law does not replace it. Instead, the Law paves the way for a good life and, in Maimonides' view, provides the best possible way to begin. Lawrence Kaplan has shown that *Eight Chapters* revolves around the relationship between obedience to the law and virtue.[9] Obedience to halakhic rules is necessary in order to instil the virtues and combat vices. It is crucial to obey the law, but doing so is instrumental. The reasons to keep the commandments go beyond mere obedience. They discipline the soul and train it to acquire virtuous character. In light of Kaplan's insight, it is worth addressing some possible objections to a system of prescribed behaviour, of which the halakha is one. The halakha, the system of ethical and ritual laws prescribed by the rabbinic tradition, presents a moral problem, since it demands obedience to an external authority. If an action is carried out purely because it is prescribed, there is no reason to think that it is a good one. For all you know, the command might have come from a malevolent being. Moreover, the law might be fulfilled out of self-interest, whether that is to receive a reward or curry favour, rather than simply because it is the right thing to do. For an action to be truly praiseworthy, it needs to be undertaken freely rather than compelled. It would make no sense to praise someone for doing something they did not choose or blame them for being forced to do something bad. Similarly, the more inclined somebody is to do something good, the more they should be praised. While that might seem an obvious claim, it could be called into question by asking whether it is more praiseworthy to act well when you have to struggle against your nature or when the good action comes naturally. It is tempting to say that someone who has to make great effort to overcome competing desires deserves more praise. After all, the actions themselves are the same, and effort to do something good ought to be recognised. However, what is ultimately more praiseworthy, in Maimonides' view, is good character. He explains comments by rabbinic sages that seem to state the opposite by saying that they refer to ritual commandments. For example, dietary laws that have no bearing on health and that in themselves are neither good nor wicked do not stem from character. 'Were it not for the Law, they would not be bad at all' (*Eight Chapters*, 80). Instead, Maimonides explains that they train character traits by teaching restraint and discipline. Transgression is associated with character traits and is therefore particularly problematic because bad character becomes ingrained and difficult to shift. The law is designed to help people master them.

The above criticisms that a commanded law is unethical are based on the idea that fulfilling the Law is nothing more than a question of obedience, but Maimonides explicitly says otherwise. He could overcome the problem because he recognises that the action itself is not what is virtuous. He writes that someone who 'merely fasts and prays' does not acquire knowledge, the human goal (1:54, 123). Therefore, actions like these are not in themselves good. They are good only inasmuch as they serve a noble purpose, which can be intermediate perfections, like acquiring virtues or perfecting society, but the ultimate purpose is human perfection, which is intellectual. I mentioned above that Maimonides considers intellectual perfection to be the way in which humans worship God. Since the law helps people to achieve that goal, it is of instrumental value. Carrying out the actions it demands is not itself true worship but, instead, leads to that worship. They are good inasmuch as they contribute to this goal. Maimonides explains a good action as follows: 'The good and excellent action is that accomplished by an agent aiming at a noble end, I mean one that is necessary or useful, and achieves that end' (3:25, 503). Even though actions are not necessarily good or bad in themselves, when considered aside from their proper ends, there are some actions that we can say are good or bad. The reason it is possible to judge whether or not an action is a good human action is that it is possible to know what a human is and therefore what the human goal is. Since humans are rational animals, the best form of life for a human is that which is conducive to actualising their rationality. An action can be good because it leads to or is conducive of this way of life. One should fulfil the law not only because it is commanded but also because it contributes to achieving the human goal.

Having said that, most of us do not always instinctively want to do what is good. We might be influenced by habits or traditions, or our physical or psychological desires. Together with the difficult subject matter and the lengthy preliminary work, these are among the impediments that Maimonides says prevent people from apprehending and studying the most advanced sciences (1:31 and 32). They can also affect our inclination to act well, not only to study. Training is therefore necessary, and ethical education is the process by which those who end up being virtuous come to understand what is truly desirable. Maimonides explains this by using the example of a child who needs to be induced to study with a reward, typically something sweet (*Commentary on the Mishnah*, 404). Before learning how to read, a child is obviously unable to appreciate the joys of reading, so cannot be motivated to learn by the activity's inherent value. Instead, they must be offered a reward, something that, in their immature state, they do consider valuable, like a sweet. When older, the child needs to be bribed with other things, like clothes or money. The aim of an education is to train people to want to do things that are valuable, like reading, not for the sake of a reward but because they are enjoyable in their own right. People who enjoy reading are disposed to read. Training character is similar, in that its aim is to encourage dispositions in people that cause them to want to do what is right.

Learning to want to do good is a process of coming to understand what is really the right thing to do and developing an inclination for it. However, inclining to the good does not necessarily mean that it is easy to carry it out. Standing up to an evil regime would take great courage and be difficult even for someone who has that virtue. What is important is not that it is easy but that it stems from her disposition. People might have natural dispositions towards matters that are not in themselves bad, but place too much importance on them to the detriment of things that are better. If I overindulge and eat too much cake, or transgress a halakhic command by giving in to the temptation to eat a cheeseburger, I might do so because it is pleasurable. In itself, pleasure is a good. Maimonides says that you sometimes need to engage in activities that are pleasurable to the senses: 'the soul needs to rest and to do what relaxes the senses, such as looking at beautiful decorations and objects, so that weariness be removed from it' (*Eight Chapters*, 77). All of these sensual activities ought to be done in service to the more important goal and a problem arises only when the pleasure gained from them is prioritised over the ultimate end. Such a confusion is a result of the character traits formed by habitual behaviour. Constantly carrying out actions that the law prescribes trains people to improve their character to a state that enables them not only to appreciate what is more important but also to be less distracted from it.

Aside from the need for practice in order to habituate ourselves to good conduct, another consequence of not knowing at the outset what actions are good is that we need someone reliable to tell us. Since people have no control over the society they are born into, and since Maimonides says that upbringing has an influence on the way we think and behave (1:31, 67), he argues that the Mosaic Law is designed to create a perfect society, inasmuch as that is possible, in order to smooth the path and provide the best possible environment to encourage developing attributes that are most truly human, those that belong to humans but not to other animals. Most people need some direction, and the Mosaic Law gives it to them. Nevertheless, it might seem that the halakha itself is not necessary for individuals to progress towards the goal, since Maimonides acknowledges that a few reached a very high degree of perfection before the law was given. He interprets the prophet Abraham as an example of someone who was able to understand truth independently simply by studying the natural world. On Maimonides' reading, Abraham grew up in a society that did not hold to an Aristotelian, scientific worldview, instead favouring astrological and magical practices, but he was nevertheless able to come to recognise the real human goal and to understand that the society in which he was raised did not promote it. Abraham even serves as a paradigmatic monotheist for Maimonides. He begins each part of the *Guide*, as well as other works, with a verse attributed to Abraham, 'in the name of God. Lord of the World' (Gen. 21:33), which he understands as Abraham's invoking God when attempting to spread monotheism and truth (3:29, 516). It is notable that Abraham lived before the Mosaic Law appeared. Obviously, he had no access to the help that the Law provides. Some rabbinic texts indicate that Abraham did indeed follow the commandments that are supposed to have been revealed to Moses at Sinai. In Maimonides' view, however, Abraham did not intuit the Mosaic commandments. He did not create a community based around something like the Law and, for that reason, did less to lead people towards their perfection. Moses put a framework in place that was designed to overcome the limitations of Abraham's approach. And, even though Maimonides sees Abraham as the figure to emulate, Abraham's relative failure helps to clarify why the halakha is so important.

David Hartman explains that 'Abraham instituted worship of God based upon knowledge. Moses was compelled to promulgate laws whose actualization reinforces and sustains this belief.'[10] In Maimonides' view, Moses understood that presenting people with philosophical arguments wouldn't get him very far. He would have been able to see that Abraham had failed to create a community that grew and lasted. Few people would be convinced purely through philosophical argument that they should live a virtuous life, dedicated to knowing science and worshipping God. There are simply too many obstacles (1:34). On Maimonides' reading, the community that Abraham built did not have the necessary bulwarks that would help people resist distracting influences and temptations. One example that Maimonides mentions is the way in which pursuing life's necessities can lead to an excessive focus on accumulating wealth. Engaging in commerce is necessary for people simply to survive. It is of greatest value when it both serves this goal and enables people to do what is truly important, which is acquiring virtues. Without the guidelines and restrictions that the

Law puts in place, the purpose can easily be forgotten, and cupidity develop, so people end up focusing on acquiring more material things instead. Maimonides writes that 'when one endeavours to seek what is unnecessary, it becomes difficult to find even what is necessary. For the more frequently hopes cling to the superfluous, the more onerous does the matter become; forces and revenues are spent for what is unnecessary and that which is necessary is not found' (3:12, 446). The halakhah helps both the individual and the community by stipulating actions that bind a society together in pursuit of virtue and also protects it against pernicious influences. In Hartman's words, 'Halakhah provides concrete symbols which remind a person of his ultimate task: to know God.'[11] Both observance and investigation are important. On the one hand, the Law is necessary for a virtuous community to preserve itself and function as it should. On the other, as Hartman explains, it is possible to become expert in legal matters while holding wrongheaded, idolatrous beliefs.[12] The aim is to unify halakhic observance, which is limited to a particular community, with intellectual contemplation, which is in principle universal.

In light of these comments about Maimonides' attitude towards Abraham and Moses, a very brief word about how he interpreted prophecy is appropriate here, although I cannot enter into detail. Maimonides considered prophecy to be a purely natural phenomenon. Once somebody has perfected their intellect, they automatically prophesy. A prophet is a philosopher, in Maimonides' view. However, prophecy is not necessarily confined to an individual's perfection. Maimonides writes that 'sometimes the prophetic revelation that comes to him compels him to address a call to the people, teach them, and let his own perfection overflow toward them' (2:37, 375). As well as perfecting their intellectual abilities, and becoming philosophers, he says that prophets have strong imaginative faculties. As explained above, imagination is concerned with material features and produces representations. These images are helpful in representing a prophecy's content to the individual prophet and the prophet is also able to use them in order to communicate with as many people as possible. Great orators know how to use similes or metaphors, and other rhetorical techniques, to persuade listeners, an important task for a prophet when teaching or leading. As a philosopher, a prophet who becomes a political leader is not interested in using power to satisfy any desire for dominion, honour, wealth, or anything else that might distract from the goal of knowing truth and worshipping God. A prophet is concerned only to create a society in which such a goal is encouraged to the highest possible degree. Maimonides claims that the Mosaic Law is divine because it is the best way to facilitate these aims. He writes that 'the Law as a whole aims at two things: the welfare of the soul and the welfare of the body' (3:27, 510). The 'welfare of the soul' consists of 'correct opinions' and 'welfare of the body' is brought about by improving the ways in which people live together. While what is termed 'the soul's perfection' is superior to the body's perfection, and therefore primary in importance, it depends on that of the body and comes about after. 'It is also clear that this noble and ultimate perfection can only be achieved after the first perfection has been achieved' (3:27, 511).

Although it is an essential characteristic of a good human life, moral virtue is not the ultimate end. It is useful because it facilitates that goal. So Maimonides writes that 'most of the commandments serve no other end than the attainment of this species of perfection. But this species of perfection is likewise a preparation for something else and not an end in itself' (3:54, 635). He views the Mosaic Law as something that provides the community and individuals with guidance as to how to live the best life. So that it can do so, he says that 'every effort has been made precisely to expound it and all its particulars' (3:27, 510). The 'ultimate end' and 'true perfection' consists in 'the conception of intelligibles, which teach true opinions concerning the divine things' (3:54, 635). The Law also includes theological doctrines, among which are those that encourage intellectual humility and pious reverence, teaching that the intellect has limitations, even while perfecting it remains the aim, and that only God is worthy of ultimate worship, even though God and the way in which God creates remain in themselves mysterious.

3

The Problem of Evil

Evil and wickedness are familiar problems to philosophy of religion students. Briefly stated, the usual form is as follows. A good agent would prevent evil as much as it is within that agent's capacity to do so. God is both good and capable of preventing any evil from taking place. Therefore, there should be no evil. However, manifestly, there is evil. In that case, one of the premises that 'God is good' and 'God is capable of preventing any evil from taking place' is false, both are false, or the argument is not valid. Since the argument is valid, one of the premises must be false. Theologians who say that God is not good are rare, and Maimonides isn't one of them (he appears not to want to accept that the proposition 'God is good' is true in any normal sense either, as I will explain in Chapter 6, but that can be set aside for the moment). It seems, then, that the second premise is false, and we are forced to admit that God cannot prevent evil altogether. If so, the incapacity might stem either from God's simply being unable to create a world without evil or from God's ignorance of evil. However, theists are generally thought to believe that God is both omnipotent and omniscient, as well as being entirely good. They are therefore apparently caught in a belief that runs counter to the evidence of human experience. Either they must deny that evil really exists or believe in an absurdity.

Maimonides considers a trap similar to the classical formulation, and argues that a number of his contemporaries fell into it. In response, he argues that they did so because they drew mistaken conclusions from the existence of evil. Evil does not show that God's knowledge is limited; instead, it shows that God's providence is limited, so those philosophers who restrict divine knowledge on the basis of evil confuse the two. His view is not an intuitive one to take, since God's providence is usually considered to be equivalent to God's knowledge. Maimonides can be seen, therefore, to question the problem. Before explaining what this confusion amounts to, however, there is much ground to cover. Maimonides' discussion of evil ranges over several topics. He attempts to explain what evil is and where it stems from, which involves discussion of the nature of matter, and also considers the goal of creation and the status of human beings. Then he embarks on his discussion of God's knowledge and providence. An extensive consideration of these issues appears in part three of the *Guide*.

As with many of the *Guide's* sections, the philosophical and theological discussions about questions related to evil are aimed not only at clarifying the issues themselves but also at enabling readers to approach sacred texts with the tools that Maimonides deems necessary to understand them properly. They are part of his project of leading people away from perplexity by explaining how to interpret biblical and rabbinic texts. Exegesis is the context for the *Guide's* chapters on evil since Maimonides interprets the book of Job as an extended meditation on suffering and divine providence, that is, on the problem of evil. Chapters 22 and 23 of part three are dedicated to Job. Maimonides cites a rabbinic statement that 'Job did not exist and was not created, but was a parable.' He then explains that 'whether he has existed or not, with regard to cases like his, which always exist, all reflecting people become perplexed; and in consequence such things as I have already mentioned to you are said about God's knowledge and His providence' (3:22, 486). Very briefly, the story's main protagonist and namesake is depicted as a pious and righteous individual, who enjoys a comfortable life. That comfort ends when Job is struck with many afflictions and begins to complain. His friends try to comfort him or explain his misfortune. Maimonides considers Job and each of his companions to be representative of a particular school of thought common in his time. Job himself thinks his afflictions unjust and therefore concludes that there is no reward for the righteous nor punishment for the wicked. One of his friends responds to the problem by saying that everything God does is just, so Job must be in some way guilty. Another argues that the purpose of suffering is to increase the reward that Job will eventually receive. Yet another claims that God wills Job's suffering but not because it is deserved, simply because God wishes it. A final opinion is put into the mouth of a character called Elihu,

and is somewhat enigmatic. It is part of what Job comes to understand at the end of the book, in Maimonides' view, which is that
human perfection lies in knowledge and understanding of God's
actions, which are the natural world. Understanding is what grants
people true happiness. Maimonides hints at this opinion in the
chapters on Job, and also at the view that human understanding
of God's purpose in creation is limited, so much so that people
only rarely fulfil their goal. How this relates to providence will be
explored below. Overall, Job teaches that evil is not good evidence
against either divine justice or reward and punishment.

It is important to note that Maimonides considered Job to be
righteous in only a limited sense at the outset. By the book's
crescendo, when Job is considered genuinely virtuous, Maimonides
says that he has changed by acquiring wisdom. He now understands
that God's purpose is unknowable and that God's knowledge and
providence are so entirely different from human knowledge and
providence that the usual responses to the problem of evil, both his
own prior opinion and those outlined by his friends, are wrong.
Instead, he now sees that his role is to actualise his human nature
as far as possible, by perfecting his intellectual virtues, not only his
moral ones. In doing so, he will understand what is truly important
and, to the extent that he successfully becomes what a human is
supposed to be, he will be covered by divine providence.

Job deals with the traditional question of a righteous person's
suffering, which raises the classical problem of evil outlined at the
start of this chapter. I will not revisit Maimonides' interpretation
of Job, but will instead explain the approach to evil that informs
his interpretation. Like the problem itself, many of the common
responses are familiar, but are often considered unsatisfying. Part
of Maimonides' general approach is among those that have at
times been widespread, that evil is a lack. This lack has its origin
in matter, says Maimonides. He begins the chapters in this section
by explaining that the source of natural things' degradation is
their matter, not their form. 'All bodies subject to generation and
corruption are attained by corruption only because of their matter;
with regard to form and with respect to the latter's essence, they are
not attained by corruption, but are permanent' (3:8, 430).

Matter is the reason that there is evil. Why should this be so? In
Chapter 2, I explained that form accounts for what something is
and matter accounts for the fact that there are many instances of
such things and that they change. Form itself does not change, but
particular existing things do. Their matter enables change because,

as Maimonides writes, 'the nature and the true reality of matter are such that it never ceases to be joined to privation; hence no form remains constantly in it, for it perpetually puts off one form and puts on another' (3:8, 431). Material things have the potential to become something different, to take on different forms. When this happens, the form that previously existed in that particular lump of matter no longer exists: the particular instantiation of the form it previously possessed is corrupted, so the generation of one thing involves the corruption of another. When compost comes into being, for example, the plants out of which it is generated cease to exist.

Since form is what makes something what it is, form is the actuality of that thing. Matter, on the other hand, being that which becomes the thing, is potency, and it is not yet that which it has the potential to be. Maimonides' philosophical tradition therefore associates matter with nonbeing. This is not to say that matter does not have being, but that a physical substance's matter is the reason that the substance lacks a feature that it might have. Its matter is the reason it is deficient. With this in mind, consider Maimonides' explanation that 'evils are only evils in relation to something; and that everything that is an evil with reference to one particular existent, that evil is the privation of this thing or of one of the states suitable for it. For this reason the following proposition may be enunciated in an absolute manner: all evils are privations' (3:10, 439). There are two interconnected points in this passage that need to be emphasised. The first is that every evil is evil in relation to something and the second is that evil is a privation. As for the first point, saying that evil is relative means that there is no existing thing that is simply bad. Badness as such does not exist in its own right. The idea can be clarified by considering evil's opposite, good. When I say that something is good, it is clear that the word's meaning depends on the kind of thing it is said of. I mean something quite different when I say that 'I am drinking a good cup of coffee' from what I mean when I say that 'I am sitting on a good chair' or that 'Superman is good.' Explaining what it is for something to be good is therefore not simply a case of coming up with a definition of good. Rather, it requires some understanding of what is described as good. The statement 'X is good' does not give you any information at all about what the X is and what 'good' means in this context, unlike 'X is yellow', which tells you that X is a certain colour and, by implication, that it is physical. You can understand the meaning of yellow independently of its bearer in a way that you can't understand 'good'. If you know that something is yellow, and you know nothing else about that thing, you know it has a certain colour and some sort of shape; if you know about something only that it is good, you don't know what sort of features it has that make it good because those features depend on the kind of thing it is. If you say that an apple is good, you mean that it is crunchy and sweet, or perhaps tart if that is your preference, but if you were to say that a doctor is good, you wouldn't be making a judgment about taste or texture. If you know what a doctor is, you know that a good doctor is skilled in the art of healing and communicating. In short, the meaning of 'good' depends on its context. Once you understand what an object is, you understand what it is to be a good instance of that object. You also know what a bad example would be, as it would be missing precisely those features that would have made it good.

With this in mind, let's consider what it means to say that evil is a privation. Fundamentally, the claim is that something is bad when it does not accord with what it is supposed to be. When something is defective, it lacks some property that a fully functioning object of that particular sort would have. So when something is considered bad because of a lack, what is missing is something that ordinarily belongs to that thing, something that follows the thing's nature. Matter is considered the source of this defectiveness; a lack in a particular individual's form depends on matter because what causes something to fail to live up to the universal form is its matter. Obviously, the individual's form cannot be the reason for an absence of that same form. A chair does not lack an aspect of what it is to be a chair because of the form of a chair, nor does a human lack something characteristically human because of human nature. They lack aspects of the form because they are hylomorphic compounds, made up of both form and matter, and their matter is what makes them susceptible to change and corruption, as matter is the source of potency for change.

Matter is the source of this lack and nonbeing because it is opposed to form, not simply because it is material. Of course, something can be bad because it lacks some necessary material, but a lack of the sort that makes something bad need not be simply an absence of stuff, as if there is some part missing that needs to be filled. It is a lack of the particular form, or of the features of that form in an individual substance. Consider a bucket, for example. It might have a hole in the side, in which case it would be deficient because there isn't enough material and adding more could patch it up. But if there is too much material, the bucket would still be deficient, although in a different way. If it is simply a solid, cylindrical piece of plastic, with a handle attached and only a small dip in the top, it would be lacking as a bucket because material needs to be removed. It lacks bucket form because there is too much, not because there is too little. Similarly, a chair could be bad because it is missing some screws. But it would also be bad if it is so big that it is fit only for giants. Such an artefact might make a good art installation, but it would not be a good chair. When Maimonides says that evil is a privation, he means that it is a lack of this kind. Nevertheless, since evil is considered a lack, there is a sense in which it is said not to exist. A bad person lacks something that is characteristic of someone who is good, like empathy. If someone lacks empathy, it simply does not exist in the person even though humans are generally by nature empathetic. So evil is simply the absence of what ought to be.

While many theologians share the opinion that evil is an ontological lack, it might be considered an unsatisfying explanation. Evil does exist, as is clear to anybody who is suffering. Of course, Maimonides and others do not claim that people are deluded when they think that they are suffering. Suffering is very real and characterising it as an ontological lack is in no way supposed to minimise that experience. When Maimonides says that evil does not exist in its own right, he is arguing that it does not exist as if it were an independent entity, not that it does not exist at all. Evil exists as a privation and is therefore distinguished from what he calls 'absolute nonbeing' (3:10, 438).

In order to begin to appreciate what Maimonides is saying here, we can consider the claim that 'exists' has different meanings. When he denies that evil is real, he is saying that one of these meanings does not apply. Sight is an oft-used example to explain the difference between something that is not at all (a wall's ability to see) and something that is, but is merely a privation (an eye's inability to see). It is true that a wall cannot see. However, it is not right to say that the wall is blind. If a person cannot see, it would be right to say that they are blind. The difference is that people have the ability to see so the blindness exists in the person. Blindness can be said not to exist in its own right, however, since blindness isn't an existing property attributed to substances, as illustrated by the fact that a wall is not blind even though it does not see. An eye is blind because it is deprived of an actuality that ought to be there given what an eye does. A privation occurs when something is lacking in the way a form is actualised in a particular material being. The blindness is real and, even though it is a privation, is said to exist because there is someone who is blind. The eye has existence and the blindness exists when the eye does not fulfil its function. When Maimonides claims that a privation does not have ontological existence, he does not deny that it exists in this way. He is saying that it exists as a lack of a certain kind. This lack is not an existing thing in its own right: it has no ontological existence. He says that those who do not recognise the difference between these two kinds of nonexistence consider evil to be caused by God. Someone who understands the difference between a privation and absolute nonexistence, and recognises that evil is a privation, will realise that God does not directly create evil. Nonexistence is not something that can be made. Therefore, God doesn't make it. Privation of sight isn't made. What is made is the eye. The reason Maimonides' analysis helps is that he is now able to argue that God does not directly create evil. He writes that God has no 'primary intention to produce evil. This cannot be correct. Rather all His acts, may He be exalted, are an absolute good; for He only produces being, and all being is a good ... Accordingly the true reality of the act of God in its entirety is the good, for the good is being' (3:10, 440). God's primary intention, says Maimonides, is to cause things that exist, and inasmuch as they exist, they are good. Nevertheless, the primary intention can have inevitable results that are not intended. If I eat a tin of peas, for example, I generate waste, but that is not my intention in opening the tin. I am simply trying to get at the peas. There could be a similarity with God's creating good and, as an inevitable result, evil coming about.

Evil has no real existence in its own right and is therefore not directly created by God, but comes into being as a side effect to God's creating something that is in itself good. Evil is merely a by-product of God's creating good. The privation itself is not caused to exist in its own right, so Maimonides says that it does not require an agent. 'Just as we say of him who puts out a lamp in the night that he has brought about darkness, we say of one who has destroyed sight that he has made blindness, even though darkness and blindness are privations and do not need an agent' (3:10, 438). On this view, God does not directly create badness. Instead, it comes about from God's causing existing things, and God's positive causality extends only to their actual being. Maimonides explains that even the existence of matter itself is in itself good, because it allows for the existence of all the forms that are generated in it.

'Even the existence of this inferior matter, whose manner of being it is to be a concomitant of death and all evils, all this is also good in view of the perpetuity of generation and the permanence of being through succession' (3:10, 440). God's goodness can therefore be defended in spite of the presence of evil in the world.

These arguments can defend the premise that God is good, even if evils come about as a result of God's activity. However, they are not enough to respond to the problem of evil since Maimonides still wishes to defend the idea that God knows human affairs. He therefore cites an argument, in the name of the philosophers, that reflects the problem and argues that God's knowledge is limited, and then he proceeds to critique it. He sums up their view like this: 'either He knows nothing at all of these circumstances, or He knows them and establishes in them the most excellent order. But we at any rate find that they are without order, do not observe analogies, and have no continuity such as they ought to have. Consequently, this is a proof that He does not know these circumstances in any way or through any cause whatever' (3:16, 462). Assuming that God is good and would therefore alleviate evil as far as possible, but that evil exists, God must be said to be incapable of preventing evil. According to this argument, that incapacity stems from ignorance of the evil that occurs to individual people. Maimonides' take on the philosophers' opinion is one shared by other theologians such as al-Ghazālī.[1] Some claim that it misrepresents Avicenna's view, but that is not the present concern. For our purposes, it is enough that Maimonides contrasts it with his own opinion, indicating that he does not consider it an adequate response. He writes that when the philosophers say that God is ignorant of individual human affairs, in order to defend God from the charge of negligence, 'they plunged into something worse than that which they tried to avoid' (3:16, 462). Maimonides objects to the philosophers' position and does not limit God's knowledge of particulars in order to absolve God of blame.

So, Maimonides presents the philosophers as saying that God cannot arrange the world to have less human suffering than the world we have, because God is ignorant of what happens to people. While he says that this position was motivated by the disorder in human affairs, he explains that philosophers justify it with a number of philosophical arguments. These arguments show that, at first sight, it seems to make sense to limit God's knowledge. In Maimonides' description, the philosophers claim that God is too exalted to have knowledge of particulars. Particular things in our world can be known only through the senses, and God has no senses, so it seems to follow that God cannot know them. Associating God's knowledge with lowly, sensual objects appears to deprecate it. God's knowledge is the most exalted form of knowledge and should therefore be universal rather than material. Furthermore, an individual simply isn't the sort of thing that can be known, if the term knowledge is strictly construed, so saying that God knows individuals does not seem to make sense. The philosophers therefore argue that 'particular things are infinite, whereas knowledge consists in comprehending; but what is infinite cannot be comprehended through knowledge' (3:16, 462). Particular things are infinite because there is no limit to how many individuals of any kind there can be, so they are potentially infinite, which is an idea I will return to in Chapter 4. Maimonides expresses the belief that the world as a whole might never cease to exist (2:27, 333). Natural kinds would therefore continue forever, and their number would be unending. Intellectual knowledge cannot encompass these particulars inasmuch as they are particular because, as explained in Chapter 2, such knowledge is said to involve knowledge of forms. The known essence, which captures the form, is common to all individuals belonging to a single kind but it does not extend to the particularities that differentiate those individuals from one another. If I know what a human is, I don't thereby know who is six feet tall and who is shorter. Their particularity is connected to their matter, and matter is not known through the intellect, since intellect is immaterial.

In sum, since God has no senses, God should not be able to apprehend particulars, and since intellectual knowledge is immaterial, it does not encompass the particulars inasmuch as they are particular, material beings. The principle lying behind both of these difficulties is that things are perceived in the manner of what is perceiving. If the intellect is immaterial, that which it apprehends can only be immaterial. Material things are therefore not apprehended by the intellect inasmuch as they are material and particular. They are grasped only inasmuch as they possess a form that is intellectually intelligible. When material beings are grasped in their particularity, they are perceived through the senses. But whereas the senses can perceive individual objects, they cannot generalise and make a judgement about all objects of the kind being sensed. For example, you can feel that Buddy the dog is furry, but you are not feeling all dogs and making a judgement that dogs are furry simply by using the sense of touch. The sense itself extends to no more than this single individual dog, so information gained through experience is limited to particular things. The philosophers argue that knowledge cannot extend to individuals because, strictly speaking, knowledge is intellectual. Instead of applying only to an individual dog, intellectual knowledge about what Buddy is applies to him and also to all other dogs of his species. It therefore makes no sense to say that individuals can be known in their individuality, together with their particular matter, rather than as part of an intelligible, universal.

In light of the philosophers' arguments, you might think that we have knowledge of particulars but that God is above that, and therefore has knowledge of universals. In order to apprehend universals, there is no need for a material organ, so God's knowledge can be universal. However, perhaps surprisingly, Maimonides says that this conclusion would diminish God. Far from distancing God's knowledge from human knowledge, those who limit God's knowledge to universals are guilty of anthropomorphising. This very attempt to remove human limitations from God's knowledge has the opposite effect, because it limits the divine to human modes of knowing. Human knowledge is necessarily limited because it cannot apprehend particular matter, which is inaccessible to the immaterial intellect. This is not to say that someone who knows what a human is doesn't also know that they have flesh and bones. People are material entities that cannot be understood without an understanding of what bones are, and understanding that humans have them. This is matter as understood but not as sensed. The matter itself cannot be understood without form, and the form is understood in an immaterial way. Additionally, the particular bones of any individual human are not part of what it is to be a human. Instead, the physical aspects are understood universally, so particulars are not said to be known in their particularity. By criticising the philosophers' approach, Maimonides can argue that God's knowledge is not restricted in these ways, even though it is not derived from senses. Unlike human knowledge, it is not limited by matter's inherent inaccessibility. Humans do not have intellectual knowledge of particulars, because intellectual knowledge is universal, and by saying that God's knowledge is limited to universals, the philosophers liken divine knowledge to human knowledge, a comparison that is illegitimate, in Maimonides' view: 'For this knowledge is not of the same species as ours so that we can draw an analogy with regard to it, but a totally different thing' (3:20, 482). This insistence on the absolute difference between human and divine knowledge is what enables Maimonides to say that God's knowledge can be unlimited in ways that human knowledge cannot.

Ultimately, Maimonides says that God's knowledge is entirely unique and is impossible for humans to understand, and he writes that, 'For us to desire to have an intellectual cognition of the way this comes about is as if we desired that we be He and our apprehension be His apprehension' (3:21, 485). Accordingly, Maimonides says only a little about God's mode of knowing. He writes as follows: 'For through knowing the true reality of His own immutable essence, He also knows the totality of what necessarily derives from all His acts.' Many questions can be raised about these claims. Considering them fully and speculating about how Maimonides might have answered them would take the discussion too far afield. Nevertheless, a couple of points can be made. Firstly, God's knowledge is self-knowledge. Therefore, since God is entirely immaterial, the divine knowledge is not at all hampered by the fact that matter is inherently unknowable. God's knowledge is therefore complete. However, Maimonides does not wish to say that God's knowledge is restricted to immaterial beings or universals. So, secondly, he also says that God knows everything that necessarily comes about as a result of the divine acts. This statement can plausibly be understood to indicate that God knows everything to which God's power to create extends. Now, if God knows creatures as their cause, and God causes matter, God knows even the aspects of individuals that depend on matter. Maimonides does not claim to know how God causes matter or how God can know that which is material, simply that God's knowledge extends not only to forms but to all that which derives from God's actions. In order to illustrate, he uses an analogy to contrast the way in which an object is known by an agent who causes it with the way in which it is known by someone who learns about it and whose knowledge is therefore derivative (3:21, 484). A watchmaker knows exactly what a watch will do without having to spend time examining it in order to work out how it behaves. Someone completely ignorant of watches would need to study it in order to understand. As usual, the manner in which any analogy must limp can cause some confusion and some have accused Maimonides of anthropomorphism. However, that is to miss the point. The analogy is supposed to show how God's knowledge is not at all limited in the same way that human knowledge is because God knows existing things as their cause. The ways in which different kinds of human perception introduce limits to how people access information cannot apply to God. Matter does not present a barrier to God's knowledge in the same way that it does to humans because God does not acquire knowledge through senses nor from an external source. Therefore, there is no need to limit God's knowledge to universals. If God knows individuals, God knows that which they lack, even if the lack itself is not a direct object of knowledge. God must be said to know the ways in which individuals can be deficient. For the purposes of his discussion of evil, the upshot is that Maimonides is unwilling to limit God's knowledge. He therefore disagrees with the doctrine he attributes to the philosophers, that God is ignorant of the affairs of individual people.

After arguing that apparent lack of order led people to deny God's knowledge of particulars, Maimonides writes that he has explained that 'the discussion concerning knowledge and that concerning providence are connected' (3:17, 464). That the discussions are connected does not mean that the doctrines are identical, and Maimonides' statement does not equate them. Instead, they are connected because providence involves questions of divine justice and human freedom, both of which Maimonides affirms, and the defence of which led the philosophers to deny God's knowledge. Maimonides needs to affirm them despite also denying the philosophers' conclusions. So, Maimonides repudiates the claim that evil shows God to be ignorant of any individuals. It does nothing of the sort, he says, but instead shows that God is not provident over all individuals. This move is unusual because God's knowledge and providence are usually thought to be equivalent, at least in extent if not intent. To understand the differences in the way Maimonides talks about them, it is helpful to think of his discussion of God's knowledge to be about God and his discussion about providence to be about creatures. More precisely, the nature of providence that extends to each thing depends on the kind of thing it is. Rather than being something inherent to God, the way in which providence attaches to things depends on the natures of those things.

I mentioned above that Maimonides interprets each of Job's friends to represent a particular school of thought. For our needs, two of those schools are relevant. One is Aristotle and the other is the Law. Maimonides writes that he agrees with much of what Aristotle has to say about the matter. He disagrees only with regard to what Aristotle says about the nature of providence that reaches humans, and even this disagreement is not total. Aristotle says that the providence covering humans is like that reaching other animals. Maimonides argues that this is not true of all humans. Some humans attain a kind of individual providence that other animals, by their very nature, cannot, although most people do not progress to these levels. I will return to the disagreements below, after explaining the part of Aristotle's opinion that Maimonides says that he agrees with.

Aristotle's view is that providence watches over everything that is permanent and unchanging. For example, Aristotle holds that God 'takes care of the spheres and of what is in them and that for this reason their individuals remain permanently as they are' (3:17, 465). However, this applies only to the heavens since no individual in our world is permanent. Individuals here can only be covered by providence to the extent that they are part of a greater whole that does not perish. A species is permanent and unchanging, so providence is said to extend to natural kinds and to ensure their survival. Providence leads to 'the durability and permanence of the species, though the durability of the latter's individuals be impossible' (3:17, 465). In our world, at the most basic level, divine providence means that all things have exactly what they need in order for the kind of thing they are to continue to exist. All individuals possess faculties that ensure the continuation of the species they belong to: 'every individual has been given that which the species he belongs to needs' (3:17, 465). Recall that the faculties of each living thing are determined by its soul. Different kinds of living things have different faculties, so some are able to fly, some are able to imagine, some are able to photosynthesise. All are geared towards their own flourishing and to continuing the species by passing on their forms to offspring. Each individual transcends itself by being part of a species, which is something permanent. The same is true of the human species. Just as a horse would need certain faculties in order to behave in a particularly equine fashion, and to generate other horses that would behave the same way, human animals need faculties that enable them to behave in particularly human ways. The practical intellect is part of what distinguishes humans, so people are 'given another faculty through which every one of them, according to the perfection of the individual in question, governs, thinks, and reflects on what may render possible the durability of himself as an individual and the preservation of his species' (3:17, 465). Humans need the practical intellect in order to survive as individuals and as a species.

So far, Maimonides goes along with Aristotle. But he says that there are two 'fundamental principles' of the Law that move him to add a major qualification. These are, one, that people have the ability to choose their actions and, two, that God grants people their just deserts (3:17, 469). In light of these principles, Maimonides seems to be faced with the problem that there are righteous people who suffer and wicked who prosper, so God does not seem to mete out justice. He cannot take refuge in saying that God is ignorant of these situations, because he insists that the philosophers were wrong to draw such a conclusion. Instead, he develops his account of providence to account for the apparent disorder in human affairs. Maimonides agrees with Aristotle that things are covered by divine providence to the extent that they are permanent. Ultimately, however, he will argue that unlike other natural kinds, humans are able to attain a degree of individual providence to the extent to which they perfect their intellects, which is to say inasmuch as they become properly human by actualising their specifically human form. Whereas other animals transcend their own individuality and become permanent by virtue of being part of a species, humans can transcend their own individuality by becoming rational, which involves understanding forms that are themselves permanent. In fact, Maimonides holds that only those who do so are fully a part of the human species, rational animals rather than brutes 'having the shape and configuration of a human being' (3:8, 433). To be truly human is to attain a degree of permanence unavailable to other animals.

To understand how his argument can work, we need to think further about the providence that extends to humans, and the providential difference between them and other animals, which is not the practical intellect. That part of the intellect does not lead to a different quality of providence. Instead, perfecting the practical intellect alone, without the speculative intellect, would enable the species to endure in much the same way as other animals do. People would be able to take care of their physical needs and reproduce, thereby enabling the animal part of the human species to be permanent. The simple fact that it is particular to humans does not mean that it enables individual providence or leads to any part of an individual acquiring permanence. The different faculties each animal has do not cause a difference in the kind of providence enjoyed but are merely appropriate and necessary in order for the species as a whole to continue. There is no providential difference between an ant and an acorn, even though their faculties differ greatly. For humans, the practical intellect allows for the same kind of providence enjoyed by other animals. This is because the difference that the practical intellect constitutes is analogous to the difference between a plant's ability to feed by growing roots and a lion's ability to feed by chasing its prey. A lion needs different faculties in order to ensure that the species lion continues. Whether or not the practical intellect amounts to a bigger difference is beside the present point. What is important is that the human animal needs to act in certain ways in order to live. These are all particularly human behaviours and therefore stem only from a human soul, not from that of a horse or a rhododendron.

As I explained in Chapter 2, Maimonides writes that humans act in a far greater variety of ways than other living beings. He gives the example of a palm, which has the single function of generating dates, and a spider, which spins webs as its distinctive activity. Similarly, swallows build and ants accumulate things. All of these have limited functions and single aims. By contrast, humans do many things that other animals cannot. Aside from the unconscious activities that they share with other living creatures, they are able to set themselves aims that are very different to one another, and which might sometimes even be in competition. Setting such goals is one of the functions of the practical intellect, which is able to learn how to build, for example, or to farm, or sew, and to invent and create tools in order to do such things. These are all necessary pursuits, if humans are to remain in existence. Taken individually, they appear to have a variety of different purposes. The farmer's goal is to generate food; the builder's is to create dwellings and storehouses and such; the tailor's vocation aims at protecting people from cold. But activities like building or sewing, or even becoming a king, do not add anything to a human's substance; they add only accidents.

As far as it relates to providence, then, the practical intellect is to humans what the faculties of other animals are to them because it enables the continuation of the species. Without it, people would be unable to carry out many essential tasks that enable them to live. It equips them to behave in characteristically human ways but it does not grant them any more permanence than that which other species have. Such actions do not yet lead to the particular kind of providence that is safeguarded to humans, since they do not lead to an individual's permanence. However, they do *allow* for that different kind of providence. The practical intellect enables the human species to endure properly as human, not only as animal, by creating conditions people need in order to actualise the other part of their intellects. Rational animals differ from other animals not only through the practical intellect but also because they have theoretical intellects. In order to be properly human, they must be 'rational' animals in the fullest sense. As I mentioned above, Maimonides claims that, unlike for the other animals, providence can extend to individual humans, and it does so to the extent that they actualise their intellects. The practical activities aim at proximate goals but, Maimonides explains, they all ultimately aim at preserving people's existence so as to perfect the single function that is the highest human goal, which is conceiving intelligibles and knowing truths. Conceiving truths adds to the essential features and transforms someone from an animal similar to others, but with a greater variety of functions stemming from a particularly human soul, into a truly rational animal. If they do not succeed in acquiring conceptions, they do not fully actualise their potential as human beings. When it comes to individual humans, Maimonides therefore writes that 'providence watches over each human individual in the manner' appropriate to that person (3:18, 475).

The way that Maimonides qualifies Aristotle's view of providence enables him to defend the Law's teaching about divine justice and affirm that there is reward and punishment. He understands reward and punishment in a fundamentally intellectual and philosophical way, and therefore distinguishes his own view from the those of 'the multitude of our scholars' and 'some of our latter-day scholars' (3:17, 469). These scholars are likewise concerned to defend divine justice and human freedom, the fundamental principles of the Law, but do so without paying attention to what the philosophers have demonstrated. They therefore misidentify the true rewards, believing that all bodily suffering is the result of a divine decree rather than an inevitable consequence of a human life. Instead, the true reward is intellectual, which is, in Maimonides' view, the most pleasurable and most permanent form of happiness, as explained in Chapter 2. To the extent that someone is truly virtuous, both rationally and morally, they receive their reward and are thereby covered by divine providence.

Maimonides argues that someone who reaches this level of providence does not suffer at all. However, that is not to say that it is possible for a human to avoid suffering or that there is anything supernatural about the process. At the end of the *Guide*, Maimonides offers a clarification 'through which doubts may be dispelled' (3:51, 624). He says that when someone is distracted from contemplating, individual providence withdraws from that person. This is when evil occurs to a person, even if the person is virtuous. Individual providence only reaches those humans who are actively engaged in the highest form of worship, which also actualises the only part of them that distinguishes them from other kinds of animals in a way that those animals are not distinguished from one another. To the extent that humans are truly righteous, by perfecting their intellectual virtues and not only their moral characteristics, and focusing on eternal truths, they are engaged in the most pleasurable activity. Such people are rewarded by providence, by achieving true human felicity, regardless of whether or not they possess the inferior goods that most believers think ought to be indicative of reward and punishment. They are rewarded by the permanence achieved by someone who engages in the highest form of human activity.

In Maimonides' view, pain that someone feels is not itself a punishment but leads to withdrawal of providence inasmuch as it distracts someone from fulfilling her intellectual goal by focusing on eternal truths, 'for it is impossible for someone to understand and reflect upon the sciences when sick or when one's limbs are in pain' (*Character Traits*, 35). Were it possible to ignore that pain, and other bodily needs, someone would 'remain permanently in that state of intense pleasure, which does not belong to the genus of bodily pleasures' (3:51, 628). However, Maimonides also writes that a permanent state of extreme perfection 'is not a rank that, with a view to attaining it, someone like myself may aspire to guidance' (3:51, 624). Suffering is a lack of providence and it is something that inevitably happens to people because they are part of the physical world. The problem of evil does not lead Maimonides to engage in a theodicy defending God's actions. Instead, it leads him to emphasise the limits of human understanding and importance. It demands a response because it has led many to draw inappropriate conclusions, that God is ignorant of individual humans, but Maimonides' solution seems no more comforting, since it involves recalibrating humanity's position in creation and accepting that only hubris makes people think that there should be no suffering or evil. People are not as important as they tend to think. Those who conclude that human suffering, especially the suffering of the righteous, indicates that God has no knowledge of particulars confuse God's knowledge with God's providence. It is not right to limit God's knowledge, says Maimonides, but providence is another matter. By emphasising that the human goal is intellectual love of God, he is able to argue that becoming properly human enables one to enjoy divine providence. Bodily suffering still happens, and it is indeed evil for the person suffering, but it is ultimately evil only inasmuch as it prevents people from being fully human. A lack of providence indicates that something is not fulfilling its potential to be permanent. The presence of evil in the world therefore teaches something about the nature of what is created, not about the nature of God or divine knowledge. And the problem of evil only arises for those who do not understand the nature of human beings and their position in the world. Because of their ignorance, they therefore conclude that physical travails should not happen to someone with good character. They do not realise that what is truly evil for humans is to fail to achieve the intellectual goal. When they are not actualising their specu-lative intellects, humans are not properly fulfilling that aspect of themselves which is permanent in itself.

Maimonides' response to suffering can be seen as a rejection of the problem of evil. He neither denies that God is purely good nor restricts God's knowledge. Since he argues that God is not ignorant of human affairs, he is unable to say that God's ignorance explains the apparently disordered circumstances in which many people find themselves. Instead, he claims that people only think that they ought not to suffer because they misunderstand the world's nature. He attempts to refocus our attention on what we are entitled to conclude from the fact that the world contains evil and asks us to reconsider the implications for our own lives. Ultimately, his answer is to say that you would only think that humans should not suffer if you have a mistaken understanding of what they are, their purpose, and their relative importance. Judged from the perspective of a single person, the entirety of creation might indeed seem to raise a problem of suffering, but Maimonides argues that God does not create for the benefit of that person, so there is no reason to conclude that God should create a world in which that individual doesn't suffer. Moreover, he even argues that judging creation from the perspective of the whole of humanity is a mistake. In creating the entire universe, Maimonides says that God's purpose cannot have been solely to benefit people. 'What is the relation of the human species to all these created things, and how can one of us imagine that they exist for his sake and because of him and that they are instruments for his benefit?' (3:14, 457). Furthermore, humans are not designed so as not to suffer. Human beings are material by nature and since matter decays so do humans. Again, rather than comparing human and divine knowledge, the more appropriate response is to recognise the limitations of human understanding.

Appreciating what humans are and their relative place in the order of creation enables people to pursue the properly human goal, which is the greatest happiness people can hope for. 'This is what one ought to believe. For when man knows his own soul, makes no mistakes with regard to it, and understands every being according to what it is, he becomes calm and his thoughts are not troubled by seeking a final end for what has not that final end; or by seeking any final end for what has no final end except its own existence, which depends on the divine will – if you prefer you can also say: on the divine wisdom' (3:13, 456).

The call to humility and understanding human limitations, including the limitations of the human intellect, is an important value in Maimonides' thought. He is sometimes said to be a sceptic, at least in the sense that he is sceptical of the human intellect's ability to know some things. Specifically, he argues that people cannot know God's essence and that they cannot be certain about some of the Law's doctrines. These include what he says about God's knowledge and also the creation of the world, which will be the topic of Chapter 4. One of my assumptions is that Maimonides would have been concerned that his opinions be coherent. On this telling, the Law's doctrines form a matrix implying one another, and are connected with his insistence that the world, including matter, is originated. However, as well as defending doctrines specifically taught by the Law, saying that God knows particulars indicates that Maimonides draws the limits around the scope of human knowledge even tighter. There are also things in the sublunar world that cannot be known scientifically. For example, in view of the claim that knowledge is fundamentally intellectual, if there are anomalies that do not follow a usual pattern, like an animal born with a defect that results from its matter rather than its form, they will not be comprehended by intellectual, universal knowledge restricted to universal forms. These features result from the matter of such things. The Law states that God is not ignorant of such anomalies, in fact knowing them as their cause. Asserting that God knows individuals as their cause, and that God causes matter, indicates that God can cause particular instances of a species to be different to how the species generally manifests. Anomalies are not simply accidents of creation, but are themselves intended. Crucially, the Law also allows for events that are absolutely unpredictable, like miracles. This is not necessarily to say that miracles have happened or will happen, simply that they cannot be ruled out and, since material beings result from

God's causative knowledge, God can create events that do not follow a usual pattern. Overall, the Law insists that our knowledge even of the world that we do understand is incomplete and so extends Maimonides' scepticism from theological concerns to natural science as well.

4

Creation and Infinity

By Maimonides' time, the question of whether the world is everlasting had been debated for centuries. Whereas the philosophers whom Maimonides most explicitly favoured maintained that the world could not have had a beginning, others had argued that since an actual infinite cannot be travelled over, and the present has been reached, the past cannot have been temporally limitless. On the one hand, a beginning to existence seems to raise the question how such a beginning could come about. On the other, if there was no beginning, and an infinite span of time needs to elapse before the present day, it seems impossible that the current time should ever come to pass. Maimonides interrogates the different opinions and presents a compelling analysis of his own. He argues that advocates of both of these views try to claim too much, if they think that reason is capable of proving the matter once and for all. He seems to think that there are worthwhile arguments for both positions or, perhaps it would be more accurate to say, there are arguments against both positions that are worth paying attention to. However, while these questions were often considered relevant to beliefs about creation, they were not always thought to be. The issue of a world without beginning is not the only important way of thinking about creation. A number of protagonists even argued that it is incidental, and that what is really important in the doctrine is not affected at all even if time had no beginning. They distinguished between different senses of creation, *ex nihilo* and *de novo*, and argued that the world is created even if it has existed forever. First, then, let's briefly consider what creation means in this context.

Philosophers in the Aristotelian tradition generally agreed that the world is somehow caused. The entirety of the world's features cannot be explained from inside the world itself. On a minimal level, the phenomenon of motion calls for explanation. Everything that is in motion is moved by something. In Chapter 2, I explained that the mover could be the thing itself, in the case of natural motion, or something external, in the case of unnatural, violent motion. Things that have no internal principle of motion would be resting, provided they are not moved by something else. There can be a chain of causes, like when someone moves a stone with a stick. The stone is moved by the stick, which is moved by a hand, which is moved by the person who can be moving herself. All such changes must end at a first mover, in this case the person, otherwise there would be no motion at all. Since motion is the actuality of something's potential to move, the world's actuality is, in an important respect, caused. There must therefore be a mover.

Imparting motion and change could easily be considered too weak an activity to amount to creation. It would not sufficiently reflect the power of a creator God. Instead, many thought that creation had to manifest God's ability to bring the world into being so that all creatures must be absolutely dependent on God for their very existence. Creation has to be *ex nihilo*, from nothing, with God the sole cause and nothing else presupposed. As stated above, even that idea could be understood in various ways, because some argued that God could, in principle, create an everlasting world with no beginning. Such a creation could still be *ex nihilo* because God uses no tool to create the world. Everything is dependent on God's existence in a way in which God is not dependent on the existence of any one of them, in a similar way to that in which rays from a bulb are dependent on and caused by the bulb's illumination but the bulb's light does not depend on the rays. Lit bulb and rays are coterminous, even though one is the cause of the other. In the case of the world as a whole, however, while such generation could be *ex nihilo*, it would not necessarily be *de novo*, since for the world to be both 'new' and 'from nothing' time itself would have needed to have an absolute beginning. Of course, the world must be dependent on God, but to count as *de novo* creation that dependence must also have begun before a finite span of time. So, some argued that the world is created, but without beginning, while others thought that such a notion was tantamount to denying creation altogether. For creation to be truly *ex nihilo*, on this view, it must also be *de novo*. A third option, which Maimonides associates with Plato, is to say that the world is created *de novo* but not *ex nihilo*, that God creates out of pre-existing matter.

This was the discussion that Maimonides was building on, and he threw in his lot with those who argued that creation ought to be understood to be both *ex nihilo* and *de novo*. In current studies, this position is sometimes expressed by saying that the world is 'originated'. It was not an obvious position to adopt, because *de novo* creation faces problems of its own. Maimonides was not satisfied with the arguments or, indeed, the world views of those who usually held this position. They are known as the Mutakallimūn, and, before embarking on a remarkable synthesis of their thought, Maimonides claims that their methodology is faulty at its root because they hold many views based on imagination rather than on intellectual reasoning. When introducing the Mutakallimūn, he explains that they build on arguments designed primarily to defend previously held opinions, rather than aiming at examining the evidence presented by the world's nature. Some of their claims are motivated by their desire 'to safeguard thereby certain doctrines of the Law that are placed under great pressure by speculation; thus the assertion in question was a way out for them' (3:15, 460).[1] Their methodology is fundamentally flawed as 'that which exists does not conform to the various opinions, but rather the correct opinions conform to that which exists' (1:71, 179). Aside from the question of whether or not Maimonides is fair to the Mutakallimūn, his assessment of their epistemology plays an important role in his arguments about creation, and I will return to his comments below.

To begin with, Maimonides holds that it can be proven, that God brings the world into being, as it follows from his view that God's existence can be demonstrated beyond doubt.[2] All should agree on the view that the world cannot account for its own existence and that it must therefore be caused to exist. I will consider Maimonides' proofs for God's existence in Chapter 5, but it is relevant that he regards a creation of this sort to follow from the philosophers' understanding of the world as well as that of the kalām. In the view of both schools, everything is brought into being by God alone. Only God is prior to everything. And since God is not something that is part of this created order, and not a thing at all, such a causality is not from any prior thing. This kind of priority need not be temporal. For example, a ring's motion is caused by that of the finger wearing it, whereas the finger's motion is not caused by the ring's. The finger moving is causally prior but not temporally prior. There is no time that the finger is moving but the ring is not, even though the ring cannot move itself. In a similar way, the world cannot cause itself, is totally dependent on God's existence, but might still exist as long as God exists. At the beginning of the *Code*, Maimonides puts it this way:

> Should one entertain the thought that God does not exist, nothing else would be able to exist. But if one entertains the thought that none of the existents aside from God exist, God alone would exist and would not be nullified through their nullification, since all the existents require God but God, who is blessed, does not require them, not a single one of them.

This statement is compatible with belief in the world's everlastingness: Maimonides does not here say that God's causality began nor does he imply that time must be finite. Some scholars claim that his position in the *Code* is more conducive to belief in the infinity of time than its finitude. A number of them then argue that Maimonides is indicating that his real opinion is in line with infinity. However, it might not indicate any such thing. Instead, his concern in the *Code* could be only to show that God exists, and is both indivisible and incorporeal, issues that are more fundamental than creation *de novo* and that, in the *Guide*, he terms 'three great and sublime problems' (1:71, 181). As I will explain further in Chapter 5, this involves providing arguments based on premises that can be accepted by those who reject *de novo* creation.[3] Moreover, even though Maimonides later says that he bases his proof in the *Code* on the premise that the world is eternal (1:71, 182), these statements are not necessarily incompatible with a beginning to time. It is true that if God is the ongoing cause of creation, and we are to assume that creation is temporally eternal, it would follow that God must also be temporally eternal. However, the converse does not follow. Simply positing that God is the eternal cause does not necessarily mean that creation is eternal. Maimonides insists that time is 'one of the created things' (2:13, 282). God's eternal existence is uncreated and therefore not temporal, so God is not forced to create an unoriginated world simply because there is no beginning to the divine being. Maimonides would have been able to assert that the world began even though there was no 'before', and that the world exists at all times even though time had a beginning.

I will say more about God's existence and attributes in the coming chapters. At this point, however, it is appropriate to mention, in passing, that there is such disagreement over the implications of the statement in the *Code* because there are so many today who do not believe that Maimonides was entirely open about what he really believed. The question of whether Maimonides was insincere is debated regarding his view of creation probably more than any other issue. Most of the secondary literature on the topic revolves around whether Maimonides is contradicting himself in order to hide his true opinion about creation. I will not be asking that question in this chapter but, instead, will explain his arguments. I am presenting here Maimonides' explicit view, which I think contains arguments worth taking seriously. Whereas some disagree, I also think that it really is the view he argues for in the *Guide*. Arguments advanced against this interpretation are either literary or philosophical, or a combination, but none of them is, in my view, satisfying. I will say more about this at the end of the present chapter, and I will address some of the reasons people argue that Maimonides' expressed opinions are, on the whole, not his real opinions in Chapter 7.

Returning to the main question, the ontological dependence of everything that exists on God is demonstrated by the proofs of God's existence but, in Maimonides' view, that does not sufficiently prove creation. Creation must be both *ex nihilo* and *de novo*. The statement in the *Code* does not require *de novo* creation, although it does not necessarily exclude it. Nor do the proofs for God's existence and unity require creation. Nevertheless, Maimonides repeatedly states that it is one of the Law's foundational teachings, even saying that 'everything is bound up with this problem' (2:26, 330). He argues that the world is created in the strong sense that time had an absolute beginning and that this opinion is a crucial foundation of the Law. If he will adopt it, though, he needs to justify doing so. This is because, by contrast with the claim that God is the cause of everything, and that creation is therefore, in the sense outlined above, proven, Maimonides says that creation in the way that he affirms it, both *de novo* and *ex nihilo*, is indemonstrable. There is no rock-solid proof that shows *de novo* creation to have either taken place or not. One of the difficulties is, I shall argue, that there is no way to conceive of it. If we cannot conceive of creation from nothing, as nothing is not a kind of thing and therefore not something of which we can have a positive conception, we are in no epistemic position either to rule it out or to assert that it is possible. Maimonides therefore cannot show that such a creation really is possible, merely that it cannot be shown to be impossible. Philosophers since Aristotle had rejected origination, so Maimonides begins on the defensive.

In order to explain his strategy, some more detail about the *Guide's* character, in addition to that given in Chapter 1, will be helpful. As well as being a work of rabbinic exegesis, the *Guide* fits into an Arabic tradition of dialectic. Dialectic is apparent both in the work's aim and in its format. The term 'dialectic' is used in various different ways. What is meant here can be traced back to Aristotelian dialectic. Aristotle addresses dialectic in the *Topics*, one of the works grouped together as logical treatises, a body of texts known as the *Organon*, an organ for thinking. As Maimonides explains, logic is the crucial first step in understanding science because it teaches you how to reason. The *Topics* deals with the rules of debate and how to win arguments. Dialectic is the practice of such arguments. Aristotle explains how to ask questions and how to respond to them, and how to prepare for a debate by, for example, thinking about who your opponent is and what premises he or she is likely to grant. One aim of a debate can be to convince an opponent that the position they advance must be abandoned, and that can be achieved in a number of ways. These include showing that the position is incoherent in itself or that it does not accord with other opinions that the opponent holds. Examining the respondent allows the questioner to draw out the implications of premises that the respondent has already granted. In this way, the questioner might be able to show that the thesis being defended implies belief in something that the defendant would not accept. If the questioner is able to evince a contradiction, the respondent is forced to concede the argument.

During a debate, it is therefore important to know what kind of evidence might count as good support for a position. Methods to convince somebody include an appeal to authority or to commonly held opinions, and the competitors have to consider the relative strengths of such claims. Logicians distinguished between demonstrative, dialectical, rhetorical, poetical, and sophistical arguments. Whereas a demonstration is a powerful argument that nobody who understands correctly would reject, a dialectical argument can be disputed. The reason is that the premises are taken from different sources from those in demonstrative proofs. Some statements are understood to be true simply by virtue of their meaning. For example, if I say that 'the whole is greater than the part', or that 'two is an even number', or that 'two things that are equal to something else are also equal to each other', anybody who understands them will accept that they are true.[4] These are known as 'primary intelligibles' or 'primary notions', primary because they are simply given to the intellect. Aristotle says that they cannot themselves be demonstrated but are accepted axiomatically. If such claims are arranged in a valid argument, the resulting conclusion must be true and someone who understands the argument correctly is 'certain' of its veracity. An argument that leads to 'certainty' is a demonstration. Together with many of his contemporaries, Maimonides also claims that healthy sense experience can provide premises for demonstrative arguments. Dialectical arguments can take the same form as demonstrative ones, but use different kinds of premises. For example, a basic syllogistic form runs as follows: A belongs to every B; B belongs to every C; therefore, A belongs to every C. If the premises are primary notions, the syllogism will be demonstrative and the conclusion certain. However, the premises might be taken from acceptable but fallible sources, in which case the syllogism is considered dialectical and the conclusion open to doubt. Acceptable premises can be 'generally accepted opinions', such as 'revealing nakedness is base' or 'excessively rewarding someone who does good is excellent'. They can also be drawn from tradition received from trusted sources.

In the argumentation theory presented in Aristotle's *Topics*, widely reputed opinions are crucial. In order to persuade someone to accept a particular claim, it can be sufficient that it be generally accepted. However, both they and traditional beliefs are sources open to doubt – contrasting views can be held in different communities – so any conclusion drawn from premises based on them would also be open to doubt. Dialectical arguments can offer evidence in favour of an opinion but they cannot show that the opinion is definitely true. Instead, they can provide evidence weaker than a demonstration. The most that can be hoped for is to come close to certainty, and al-Fārābī, whose logical works were an important source for Maimonides, writes that 'assent that approximates certainty is dialectic verification'.[5]

While it is useful for the debating chamber, Aristotelian dialectic also aids science. Testing someone else's arguments is similar to testing a scientific hypothesis. Dialectical examination can clarify exactly what the argument in a claim's favour amounts to, whether it is valid, and what the assumptions underpinning it are. It is also useful for drawing out the consequences of premises in order to work out whether or not they might be acceptable. Maimonides' arguments about the world's everlastingness take place against this background. He uses dialectic to defend his position, but he is not merely involved in a debating game. Instead, he examines the arguments in favour of the different positions and draws out their consequences. First of all, he presents the different possible views about whether the world is everlasting and examines them in order to show what they entail. Secondly, he argues that this is a realm concerning which there can be no certainty. Any proof, whether or not it is true, can only show that it is either likely or unlikely, not that it is true beyond all doubt. There are no demonstrative arguments that can show whether or not the world is everlasting and Maimonides spends a good deal of time trying to show the limitations of those who argue that there are. In such a case, he states that 'it is preferable that a point for which there is no demonstration remain a problem or that one of the two contradictory propositions simply be accepted' (2:16, 293). If a decision between alternative possibilities is to be made in such cases, there is no choice but to rely on less than certain premises. Maimonides must therefore argue that the Aristotelian attempts to prove that creation is impossible do not amount to a demonstration.

Let's first consider what it could mean to say that the cosmos is infinite. Trying to conceive of infinity can be mind boggling. In the modern period, our ability to do so has been revolutionised but, long before, problems were pondered and alternative explanations offered. For medieval theologians, the question of infinity had important ramifications. It was common to distinguish between a potential infinite and an actual infinite. Infinity could be said to exist potentially. Numbers can be multiplied or divided indefinitely. The infinite division is not actual, however. Its existence is posited only because no limit can be placed on how many divisions there could be. The same is true of additions: no matter how high a number you posit, it is always possible to add another. An actual infinite existing all at once was thought to be a different matter. Consider an infinite body, for example. Maimonides states that 'the existence of any infinite magnitude is impossible' and also that 'the existence of magnitudes of which the number is infinite is impossible – that is, if they exist together' (2: Introduction, 235). Bodies by nature have three dimensions, and are surrounded by other bodies. None of them is, individually, boundless. This follows from their definition. A body is in a particular place and moves relative to other bodies. Place must be distinct from space in order for it to be possible for a body to move around and occupy a different location. Can the same be said of the total aggregate of bodies? A positive answer would raise the question of what is outside the mass of bodies. Aristotle and his followers argued that body is coextensive with dimension, so there cannot be something that is not a body but which, nevertheless, occupies space. Does the universe therefore extend indefinitely? Later scientists would go on to argue that space and body do not have to be equivalent to one another in extent, so they considered space to be infinite even if body is not. Maimonides, however, followed the scientific orthodoxy of his time and claimed that the universe must be limited. On this view, it would not make sense to argue that there is infinite body, since all body must be contained.

One might think that similar reasoning applies to time and some argued that it did. If time is infinite, it can have no end point. Since it appears to have a boundary, as we have arrived at the present, time cannot be infinite. Many philosophers were not convinced. The reason that arguments against an actually existing infinite apply to body but not to time, says Aristotle, is that time is infinite in a potential rather than an actual way. He says that time is a number of motion that depends on a difference between an earlier state and a later one. Maimonides sums up the view pithily in the following way: 'Time is an accident consequent upon motion and is necessarily attached to it. Neither of them exists without the other. Motion does not exist except in time, and time cannot be conceived by the intellect except together with motion' (2: Introduction, 237). There are two crucial things to note here. One is that time depends on motion and the second is that the intellect is dependent on this motion in order to notice time. An actual stretch of time depends on someone counting it by noting a starting point and an end. Time is what passes in between these two moments. A moment is defined as the limit in a similar way to how a point is the limit of a line. A line can be divided at any of its points, but the points do not in themselves exist unless the line is so divided. They exist potentially. The line can potentially be extended to infinity, since at any point, more can be added. The same can be said of time. Whichever moment you choose, it is possible to go further. To posit an everlasting world is to say that you will never reach the end of this series, no matter how far back you go. Therefore, by contrast with a universe of unlimited size, it is possible to posit an everlasting world, since the infinite involved would be only potential.

Maimonides agrees, and he therefore adopts the view that an infinite world cannot be ruled out. However, in his presentation, which accords with a commonly held interpretation, Aristotle

goes further and argues that it is not only possible, but true, for
a beginning is impossible. Maimonides responds by adopting
a dialectical stance. He begins the chapters that he dedicates to
arguing for creation with explanations of three common theistic
approaches to origination. Recall that in its most basic sense,
creation is proven if God's existence is proven. However, this is
not the sense that Maimonides argues about. Since Maimonides
will argue that God's existence can indeed be proven, he says that
he is entitled not to consider those who do not believe that there
is a God. Instead, the question he considers in this context is the
nature of creation. The first position is that of the Law, which posits
an absolute beginning, that the world was created out of nothing
'from absolute nonexistence'; the second is attributed to Plato,
and consists in the belief that time did not begin, that matter is
everlasting, but that God forms different things out of it, 'sometimes
a heaven and earth and sometimes something else'. On this view,
God's causality is similar to that which a potter has to clay, says
Maimonides, inasmuch as the clay is receptive to the form imposed
by the artist. The world that we have may not be everlasting, but it
is preceded by other material things. 'For it is generated and passes
away just as the individuals that are animals are generated from
existent matter and pass away into existent matter. The generation
and passing-away of the heaven is thus similar to that of all the
other existents that are below it' (2:13, 283). The third position is
Aristotle's and that of his followers. Aristotle agrees with Plato that
time cannot begin, and that something material cannot come about
unless it is preceded by matter. He adds that the world has always
behaved in the way it does now and always will do. It is necessary
because it is an automatic result of God's existence and therefore
cannot fail to exist. Just as steam would necessarily rise in the
absence of an impediment, God necessarily creates. Furthermore,
since Aristotle holds that the world must always behave in the
same manner as it does now, his view rules out the possibility that
the creator can particularise the individuals. The account of God's
knowledge in Chapter 3 is therefore relevant, and I'll say something
more about the connection when I introduce Maimonides' reasons
for preferring origination.

So there are three opinions that Maimonides deems worthy of
consideration. For now, they can be divided into two parties, and
the question that separates them is whether or not time began:
'there is, in our opinion, no difference between those who believe
that heaven must of necessity be generated from a thing and pass

away into a thing or the belief of Aristotle who believed that it is not subject to generation and corruption' (2:13, 285). Actually, Maimonides' attitude to Plato seems ambivalent, and I'll return to it below. At the moment, what is important is that both groups of philosophers agree about the principle that existing things must be preceded by existing things: 'it is absurd that God would bring a thing into existence out of nothing' (2:13, 282) and 'something endowed with matter can by no means be brought into existence out of that which has no matter' (2:13, 284). For our purposes, they can be said to reject creation *ex nihilo*. Asserting that something can come to be from absolutely nothing is, they claim, a logical impossibility.

> To predicate of God that He is able to do this is, according to them, like predicating of Him that He is able to bring together two contraries in one instant of time, or that He is able to create something that is like Himself, may He be exalted, or to make Himself corporeal, or to create a square whose diagonal is equal to its side, and similar impossibilities. What may be understood from their discourse is that they say that just as His not bringing impossible things into existence does not argue a lack of power on His part – since what is impossible has a firmly established nature that is not produced by an agent and that consequently cannot be changed – it likewise is not due to lack of power on His part that He is not able to bring into existence a thing out of nothing, for this belongs to the class of all the impossible things. (2:13, 283)

The first task is for Maimonides to explain and respond to the Aristotelian view that the world had no beginning, and that to posit a beginning is to posit a logical absurdity. He cites several arguments in Aristotle's favour. These arguments have their starting points either in Aristotle's teachings about the nature of the world or in what he says about God. To be more precise, Maimonides states that the physical arguments, those derived from the world, are taken from Aristotle, whereas the 'theological' arguments were based on his principles but expounded by some of his followers. I will not explain all the arguments in this chapter, both because of the space it would take and because Maimonides' overall claim can be elucidated without doing so.[6] Instead, I will consider the physical arguments, since it is they that lead to the alleged absurdity of the sort mentioned in the above quotation. By contrast, arguments stemming from assumptions about God's nature are supposed to lead to positing incongruities of God, such as change or inability. Maimonides responds that change in creation does not imply change in God. Like the philosophers' statements about God's knowledge that were considered in Chapter 3, these arguments assume a similarity between our activities and God's. Above, the philosophers' claim was that if God knows things that change, there is a change in God's knowledge between two different times. Maimonides answered that a change in the state of created affairs does not necessarily entail a change in God's knowledge, since God's knowledge of created affairs is causative. In the case of creation, their claim is that changing from not creating to creating is a change in God. In response to this, too, Maimonides argues that creation does not require God to change. Because time depends on change, there cannot be time before creation, which means that there was no time at which God was not creating. To say otherwise would be to imply that God is subject to time, which is something Maimonides denies when he states that time is created. Again, then, the philosophers' arguments based on the nature of God stem from an anthropomorphism and from paying insufficient attention to what it means to say that God is transcendent.

To return to the physical arguments, Maimonides explains that any idea that motion began 'in an absolute sense' contravenes the basic Aristotelian account of nature. There are a number of arguments to this effect and, in Maimonides' view, all of them attempt to frame an absolute beginning in the same way as the beginning of something that is part of the observable world. Consider one of the arguments he reports, for example, which argues that anything produced in time is preceded by the possibility of its generation. Were it impossible, it would not have been able to come about, but it evidently has. Nor can it be necessary. Had it been necessary it would already have existed. Since necessary, impossible, and possible exhaust the alternatives, the thing itself must have been possible. The possibility must itself have resided in some substratum, such as another material being. Without that prior existing potentiality, the new thing would not have been possible. I can only make a statue, for example, if there is a block of material out of which to fashion it. This reasoning can be applied to the world as a whole and is then, Maimonides says, 'a very powerful method for establishing the eternity of the world' (2:14, 287). The nature of time also seems to prohibit any thought of it beginning. Given that a moment is defined as a limit, it necessarily has a before and an after. A first moment cannot occur, by definition, since, as above, the moment must always be preceded by a previous time. It seems, then, that the very meaning of a moment rules out any possibility of an absolute beginning to time.

Maimonides agrees with Aristotle's account of time and of how the world we experience works: 'Everything that Aristotle has said about all that exists from beneath the sphere of the moon to the centre of the earth is indubitably correct' (2:22, 219). However, he argues that Aristotle's investigations in natural science are not relevant to the question of creation. His teachings about the nature of time simply would not hold in the case of an absolute beginning. If a moment is defined as a limit between before and after, an absolute beginning does not conform to the definition of a moment because, in the case of an absolute beginning, there is no before. Therefore, even if every moment is by definition preceded by some time, it would not follow that an absolute beginning must be. Maimonides cannot have understood creation from nothing to be creation at a first moment since an absolute beginning would not answer to the definition of a moment. Definitions that apply to the world as it is do not necessarily apply to creation, because creation is not an event comparable to anything that takes place in nature. Maimonides therefore responds to arguments against creation, and writes that 'this contention cannot be proved to be impossible by inferences drawn from the nature of what exists' (2:17, 298).

There is an analogy with natural generation, in the difference between an animal's natural operations and the way in which it comes to be. In order to live and grow, a person needs to eat and breathe, but it does not follow that a foetus does either of these activities. Maimonides explains that 'no inference can be drawn in any respect from the nature of a thing after it has been generated, has attained its final state, and has achieved stability in its most perfect state, to the state of that thing while it moved toward being generated. Nor can an inference be drawn from the state of the thing when it moves toward being generated to its state before it begins to move thus' (2:17, 295). He then asks us to imagine a man whose mother died shortly after his birth, and who has spent his entire life on an island, never seeing a female of any species. If the nature of a human gestation period is explained to him, he would consider it absurd, and would argue on the basis of his experience. 'He will say: if any individual among us were deprived of breath for the fraction of an hour, he would die and his movements would cease. How then can one conceive that an individual among us could be for months within a thick vessel surrounding him, which is within a body, and yet be alive and in motion?' (2:17, 295). All arguments that the man offers would make perfect sense on the basis of his experience, but they fail because they push his limited perspective beyond its boundary, like those who argue against creation on the basis of the way the world behaves.

Of course, the analogy ultimately limps because there is still a time before someone is born, and is in the process of being generated, and there is prior material out of which someone comes to be. Maimonides is obviously aware of the ways in which the analogy differs from that which it is an analogy for. He points out that there can be no 'before' the world if creation is *de novo* and *ex nihilo*:

> Accordingly, one's saying: God 'was' before He created the world – where the word 'was' is indicative of time and similarly all the thoughts that are carried along in the mind regarding the infinite duration of His existence before the creation of the world, are all of them due to a supposition regarding time or to an imagining of time and not due to the true reality of time. For time is indubitably an accident. According to us it is one of the created accidents, as are blackness and whiteness. (2:13, 281)

What is important in an analogy is what it serves to clarify, and the point is clear. Simply observing an animal's everyday behaviour doesn't give you information about what it is like 'while it moved toward being generated' nor about what happened 'before it begins to move thus'. Similarly, observing the way the world works now does not give you any information about whether or not it came to be. If origination is out of nothing, there is no way to compare it to events in the world, and it is not something we can experience or encounter. It therefore cannot be deemed impossible simply because it is completely unlike the kinds of generation that we are able to witness.

Here, it is worth asking why we might judge something to be impossible, and there could be several different reasons. There is a difference between something that is impossible because it is inconceivable and something impossible because it is nonsense. It is a theme that Maimonides returns to later in the *Guide*.[7] Regarding the particular question of creation, he argues that philosophers who argue that origination is impossible try to stretch their reasoning further than it can go. Remember that when he introduces the belief that time could not have a beginning, he describes it as a claim that to assert a beginning is like bringing together two contraries, a logical absurdity. God could no more create the world *ex nihilo* than create a square circle. Maimonides states that all agree that God cannot do what is impossible, and denying that he can is not to place a limit on divine power. There is a disagreement over what is logically possible because people disagree on the criterion for deciding: 'the power over the maker of the impossible is not attributed to the deity. This is a point about which none of the men of speculation differs in any way. And none but those who do not understand the intelligibles, is ignorant of this. The point about which there is difference of opinion among all the men of speculation concerns a certain species of imaginable things' (3:15, 459). Those matters that are both inconceivable and unimaginable are agreed by all to be impossible.

The argument between Aristotle and the kalām regarding creation is therefore over whether or not it is conceivable. Aristotle argues that it is inconceivable and therefore impossible. Kalām thinkers argue that it is conceivable and therefore possible. Their criteria for conceivability differ: for Aristotle intellect and for the kalām imagination. Throughout the *Guide*, Maimonides stresses his general agreement with the philosophers. His disagreement on this question does not signal a sudden switch to kalām methodology even though he agrees with their conclusion. Rather, he continues to disagree with kalām methods but argues that the philosophers too are in no position to judge the matter. While he agrees with the philosophers' method for deciding what is intellectually conceivable, he does not agree that the inconceivable is automatically impossible. That would depend why it cannot be conceived. To say that something is inconceivable is not necessarily to say that it is absurd.

In a passage that echoes the earlier statement, Maimonides writes as follows:

> Similarly, the bringing into being of a corporeal thing out of no matter whatever, belongs – according to us – to the class of the possible, and to the class of the impossible – according to the philosophers. The philosophers say similarly that to bring into being a square whose diagonal is equal to one of its sides or a corporeal angle encompassed by four plane right angles and other similar things belong all of them to the class of the impossible; and some of those who are ignorant of mathematics and, concerning these matters, know only the words by themselves and do not conceive their notion, think that they are possible. (3:15, 460)

Again, the philosophers argue that creation from nothing is as absurd as 'a square whose diagonal is equal to one of its sides'.

Anyone who understands what a square and a diagonal are would agree that this is impossible. It can neither be conceived nor imagined, so the philosophers are likening it to a logical impossibility that all ought to reject, like a square circle. The reason for their view is that they are judging creation on the basis of what the intellect can grasp. Although you can't conceive of such a square, you know what a square is and you also know what a diagonal is, so you can understand why it is impossible. On this view, if the intellect is incapable of depicting something, it must be impossible. However, this is a mistake because it does not attend to different reasons that the intellect might fail. If creation *ex nihilo* cannot be understood for the same reason a square circle cannot be understood, there would be a case for saying that it is impossible. Since the reason is different, however, the judgement cannot be made on the same basis.

So creation from nothing is inconceivable for a different reason than that which renders a square circle inconceivable. In the case of a square circle, we know what a square is and we know what a circle is. Even if they are in the external world, they are both human concepts and can be contrasted. Putting together two distinct concepts in the same category is meaningless because asserting one involves denying the other. In this case, square and circle are being combined even though we can say that they are different things. We can see why squares cannot be circles, because we know that they are different kinds of shapes. A shape that is square excludes a shape that is circular. The case differs from putting together things from separate categories, like substance, quantity, and quality. Unlike a circular square, you can talk about a large or small square, or a red or green square, because there is no opposition between substance and attribute. Now, if origination is comparable to a square circle, and therefore logically impossible, origination must involve bringing together two things that we know cannot be combined. Indeed, it appears at first sight to do so, because all generation occurs from something that previously existed but had the potentiality to change. The phrase 'something from nothing' therefore seems similarly absurd since it too is inconceivable, as Aristotle's arguments make clear. If so, in the same way as a square circle has no meaning, creation from nothing would also have no meaning because 'something' and 'nothing' would be opposed to one another in the way that 'square' and 'circle' are opposed to one another. However, it cannot be ruled out in like fashion, for the reason it is inconceivable differs. Whereas both circle and square are conceivable in themselves, 'nothing' is not conceivable at all. Since we do not have any concept of absolutely nothing and the way in which it opposes 'something', if at all, we are not in a position to judge that the difference between 'something' and 'nothing' mirrors the opposition between 'square' and 'circle'. We are therefore not in a position to say that 'something from nothing' is self-contradictory and absurd. As Maimonides explained in the chapters on creation, the categories that describe parts of the created world simply do not apply to creation as a whole, and he asserts that the philosophers are therefore mistaken to rule out origination as if it is a logical impossibility.

So, Maimonides' point is that the arguments designed to show that an absolute beginning is impossible are flawed. We cannot know that such a beginning is impossible. But can we know that it is possible? Maimonides argues that such knowledge is also beyond our ken. Those who claim that it is possible, he says, base a number of their fundamental scientific opinions on imagination rather than intellect. Maimonides writes that the imagination is only capable of dealing with material beings (1:73, 209) and, since imagining something that is a body automatically entails imagining something with physical dimensions, the image would include accidents of quantity. 'For the imagination apprehends only that which is individual and composite as a whole, as it is apprehended by the senses; or compounds things that in their existence are separate, combining one with another; the whole being a body or a force of the body. Thus, someone using his imagination imagines a human individual having a horse's head and wings and so on' (1:73, 209).

The imagination combines impressions gained from sense experience in creative ways and is capable of generating images that do not depict anything existing in external reality. When operating in this way, the imagination can combine attributes that do not belong together. Nonetheless, Maimonides reports that the kalām consider the imagination to be the proper judge of what is possible (1:72, 206). Their claim is that if you can imagine something, God can create it: if something can exist in the imagination, denying that God can create it in the physical world would be setting a limitation to God's power. This leads them to assert that certain imaginable situations are possible. The debate is not over whether a square circle is possible, since, besides being inconceivable to the intellect, it is also unimaginable. Because the imagination deals in material beings, such an object cannot be depicted there. As he stated in a quotation above, the debate 'concerns a certain species of imaginable things'. In this case, Maimonides sides with the philosophers and argues that the imagination cannot judge the matter. It is impossible, for example, that the flower on my windowsill is currently looking out of the window, even though it could be portrayed to be doing exactly that. Accidents can be imagined in inappropriate substances and flowers might look out of windows in stories or cartoons. The reason that this is impossible is that looking is not the kind of activity that flowers undertake, so the combination of the two is nonsense even if it can be imagined. Given that the object in question is a flower, and flowers do not see, sight cannot be predicated of it. This example illustrates that the range of predicates that can be sensibly applied to any subject depends on the kind of thing it is. The subject's form is restrictive, as well as being that which actualises the thing, since a particular form excludes certain kinds of properties. A thing cannot be both a flower and a human being, unless one of the two is given a metaphorical meaning, so attributing the form of flower to a particular lump of matter excludes the form of human from that same matter. Like denying that a square is a circle, affirming that a thing is a flower involves denying that it is a human, a horse, a piece of cheese, or any other non-floral substance. It also excludes properties that could sensibly be ascribed to humans or horses but not to flowers. Excluding accidental properties in this way involves positing a relative sort of impossibility, which depends on the kind of substance that the accidents are assigned to, rather than an absolute impossibility. The activity of seeing is impossible only in relation to the subject it is predicated of, if that subject is not the kind of thing that can be seeing or blind, but the activity is not impossible in itself. The conceptions 'flower' and 'sight' are intelligible, unlike squares with diagonals equal to one of their sides, but their combination is impossible so it cannot be acknowledged to be true.

When the kalām argue that origination is possible, they claim that it is imaginable. Can a genuine origination be imagined? The imagination is able to combine substances and accidents perceived by the senses and depict objects such as a flea-sized elephant. In doing so, it combines different categories, substance and size, in a fictional way. One of the reasons it is able to do so is because there is no opposition between the two parts of the combination. It is normal for a substance to be of a certain size, even though elephants are not the size of fleas. The kind of impossibility that is created by the imagination differs from the intellectually inadmissible round square. The tiny elephant would be more like imagining a giant football the size of the sun, or a match between miniature players taking place in a plant pot. And, whereas the tiny elephant and giant football can be imagined, because a substance could indeed be small as a flea or large as a star, the round square cannot because both are shapes. They are in the same category and to affirm one would involve denying the other since to be a circle means to be something different from a square; it would involve the claim that a circle is not a circle. The kalām agree that such a thing would be impossible as it cannot be depicted in the imagination. These examples are different from those that could be compared to creation, they say, as imagining creation would involve a change, specifically from nonbeing to being, rather than a combination of diverse attributes into a single substance. Instead, it would be closer to a generation of one thing from another thing. For example, the imagination could depict a rose bush growing from an apple seed. Although impossible, this is a change from one thing that can be imagined, because of its matter, to another that can also be imagined.

Kalām theologians think that they are relying on the imagination in order to argue for creation, but Maimonides argues that they are mistaken because they are not really arguing for creation at all. If, as he says, the imagination cannot free itself from matter, every generation that the imagination depicts must be from a prior existent matter. Additionally, when criticising the kalām reliance on imagination, the examples that Maimonides uses to illustrate the false images it generates do not seem to correspond to a creation from absolutely nothing. When the kalām judge creation to be possible, the creation that they posit must be imaginable. But in this case, they are not imagining creation *ex nihilo* but, rather, a creation from relative nonbeing. If absolute nothingness genuinely involves no matter at all, and the imagination deals only with material things, absolute nothingness cannot be imagined. Since the kalām say that only what is imaginable is possible, the sort of creation they are able to posit must therefore be a creation from relative nonbeing. In sum, even if one were to accept the principle that what is imaginable is possible, the kalām would be unable to establish their claim that origination is possible. The imagination is only able to depict material realities, and is therefore unable to judge whether the world could possibly not exist. It cannot affirm an absolute beginning, because it is unable to form a picture of absolute rather than relative nonexistence. An absolute beginning is no more imaginable than it is intellectually conceivable.

Maimonides states that Aristotle's arguments succeed against the kalām but not against his own position: 'For these arguments necessarily concern only those who claim that the stable nature of that which exists gives an indication of its having been created in time. I have already made it known to you that I do not claim this' (2:17, 296). He says that Aristotle is right to argue against the idea that origination can be proven to be true. 'For he has inferred from the nature of motion that motion is not subject to generation and passing-away. And this is correct. For we maintain that after motion has come into existence with the nature characteristic of it when it has become stable, one cannot imagine that it should come into being as a whole and perish as a whole, as partial motions come into being and perish' (2:17, 297).

Since there are no other ways to assess whether something is impossible, aside from using intellect or imagination, Maimonides asks 'is there something that shuts and blocks this gate so that a man can assert decisively that such and such a thing is impossible because of its nature? Should this be verified and examined with the help of the imaginative faculty or with the intellect? And by what can one differentiate between that which is imagined and that which is cognised by the intellect? ... Is there accordingly something that permits differentiation between the imaginative faculty and the intellect? And is that thing something altogether outside both the intellect and the imagination, or is it by the intellect itself that one distinguishes between that which is cognised by the intellect and that which is imagined?' (3:15, 461). He offers no answer, simply stating that 'All these are points for profound investigation.'[8]

On the reading advanced in this chapter, Maimonides says that neither the imagination nor the intellect is capable of judging creation *de novo* to be possible or impossible, because neither can properly depict it. While the philosophers are right to object to the kalām accounts of what is possible, which are based on imagination, they are mistaken to liken origination to a square circle. If it is indeed impossible, it cannot be shown to be impossible in the same way. Whereas square and circle can be both conceived and imagined independently, but not in combination, 'nothing' can be neither conceived nor imagined. Maimonides therefore has no criterion for judging whether creation *ex nihilo* is possible. Neither imagination nor intellect will do the job. Human perceptual and analytical apparatus cannot portray it. Nor can they rule it out because they cannot even depict all of its elements. So, while we cannot depict a square circle because we can know it to be absurd, our inability to depict creation from nothing differs because it is down to the fact that we are not in an epistemic position to do so.

Until now, I have presented Maimonides as arguing that human faculties cannot decide either in favour of one or the other of the two alternatives, a world without beginning or a creation *de novo* and *ex nihilo*. However, he goes on to argue that there are good reasons to accept that origination is true. Among these reasons, some are theological and some are scientific. The theological proofs indicate that God creates with will and purpose, and the scientific evidence backs this up. Nevertheless, Maimonides does not violate his claim that creation cannot be depicted even though he asserts its truth. The reason is that the evidence he offers is not directly concerned with conceptualising origination. Instead, he relies on prophetic tradition, which he says 'should not be set at nought' (2:17, 294), and elaborating the consequences of opting for one view or the other. Once those consequences are understood, he is able to consider what the tradition teaches about them. Furthermore, he is also able to examine certain phenomena in the created world and consider whether they appear to fit better with one of the two opinions.

Understanding the nature of scientific enquiry and the role dialectic has to play is crucial. Maimonides reports that ignorance of the difference between demonstration and dialectic is a cause of major error in understanding arguments about the world's temporal origination (1:71, 180). It is a charge that he attempts to level at all who think that they have demonstrated the matter one way or the other.

> The majority of those who consider themselves as perspicacious, even though they have no understanding of anything in the sciences, decide simply that the world is eternal through acceptance of the authority of men celebrated for their science who affirm its eternity, whereas they reject the discourse of all the prophets, because their discourse does not use the method of scientific instruction, but that of imparting reports coming from God. Only a few favoured by the intellect have been guided aright through this second method. (2:15, 293)

Maimonides here characterises those who think that eternity is demonstrated as followers of Aristotle who did not properly understand him. Aristotle himself, in Maimonides' view, made no such mistake. He knew that there is no demonstration, but he did not have access to all of the evidence that Maimonides uses.

Whereas Aristotle had no reliable tradition teaching origination, Maimonides argues that the rabbinic tradition does teach it, and he insists that prophetic reports should be taken into account. He stresses that this is not a question of taking the bible literally. 'Know that our shunning the affirmation of the eternity of the world is not due to a text figuring in the Torah according to which the world has been produced in time' (2:25, 327). In fact, he states that some have been misled into believing in an everlasting world by unquestionably accepting the literal sense of certain biblical statements (2:30, 349). He also writes explicitly that the texts should not be understood literally on this point (2:17, 198). Why, then, does he argue that origination is important? He makes the following remark about Aristotle's view:

> the belief in eternity the way Aristotle sees it – that is, the belief according to which the world exists in virtue of necessity, that no nature changes at all, and that the customary course of events cannot be modified with regard to anything – destroys the Law in its principle, necessarily gives the lie to every miracle, and reduces to inanity all the hopes and threats that the Law has held out. (2:25, 328)

In Chapter 3, I explained that God should not be denied knowledge of particulars on the basis that they are material, since God knows them as cause. I also mentioned that Maimonides argues that his opinion is not certain and that God's knowledge of particulars is what allows for the Law's doctrines. Like creation, it is something that he can argue for only on a dialectical basis. It is this view, that God knows particulars, and therefore is able to particularise them without thereby rendering them necessary, that allows for belief in miracles. Since God knows creatures as their cause, that discussion is connected with creation, and the Law's doctrines create a web of mutually implicating beliefs. And, since Aristotle's brand of eternity is, in Maimonides' presentation, incompatible with these beliefs, it ought to be rejected. Maimonides therefore writes the following, to conclude his chapters on divine knowledge. 'With regard to all problems with reference to which there is no demonstration, the method used by us with regard to this question – I mean the question of the deity's knowledge of what is other than He – ought to be followed. Understand this' (3:21, 484).

On this question, Maimonides' ambivalence to Plato emerges. Regarding the possibility of an absolute beginning, he aligned Plato with Aristotle, since both considered it impossible. Here, however, he accepts that Plato's opinion would be acceptable from the perspective of the issues he addresses now. If Plato is right, God is able to create a world to have one set of particular features or another set, since God is able to fashion existing material according to the divine will and purpose. Maimonides writes that 'the true reality and quiddity of will means that someone can will and not will' (2:18, 301). If God creates through will, God is not compelled by nature or an external force but is free to create according to the divine purpose or even not to create at all. Plato's view is therefore acceptable inasmuch as it is compatible with God's knowledge of particulars and ability to create a world without necessity. It is compatible with holding that one cannot rule out God's ability to introduce a particular difference that science, because it deals with universals rather than particulars, cannot predict.

One response could be to argue that Plato's view is the most acceptable since it accords with the view that a completely mysterious beginning is impossible but also recognises that the rules of physics that apply within the world do not have a bearing on how to think of the world as a whole coming into being. While it has been suggested that Plato's view is actually the one that Maimonides favours, it is not his professed opinion and he argues against it explicitly.[9] Indeed, since Plato agrees with Aristotle that an absolute beginning is impossible, he attempts to push the arguments from natural science beyond the bounds that Maimonides marks out. Plato's belief is therefore also subject to Maimonides' arguments about the limitations of science. If Maimonides' case against the demonstrative force of Aristotle's arguments succeeds, it also establishes that there is no reason forcing us to accept Plato's opposition to an absolute beginning. Maimonides draws tighter limits than does Plato around our understanding of how God creates. As above, he argues that there is no evidence that enables us to rule out origination, and so Plato's confidence that it is impossible is unwarranted. Maimonides' opposition to eternity stems not only from his claim that it destroys the Law but also from his arguing that it asserts more than is humanly knowable about God, which is that God cannot create a world in any way different from the present one. 'For in this opinion is contained the destruction of the foundation of the Law and a presumptuous assertion with regard to the deity' (2:23, 321). They presume to know that God cannot create the world through will and purpose and, consequently, is unable to create a world from absolute nonexistence.

What about the scientific arguments in favour of God's creating through will and purpose? These are based on astronomical observations, and Maimonides says that they 'come close to a demonstration', which, as I mentioned above, is a recognised way of saying that they are dialectical. In this case, too, Aristotle deserves no blame for not attending to the evidence, since Maimonides reports that 'the science of astronomy was not in his time what it is today' (2:19, 308). Again, Aristotle simply did not have access to the evidence Maimonides proffers. In order to follow his reasoning here, we must do so with a medieval picture of the universe in mind. He describes a simple version at the beginning of the *Code* in which he explains that the earth lies at the centre of a series of concentric spheres, each surrounded by another, with no gaps between them, 'like the layers of an onion'. Each sphere contains a planet or, in the case of one of them, a number of stars. These are known as 'animated' spheres. Nine of these spheres were posited, and they were thought to be constituted of a fifth element, a quintessence, known as aether. This different kind of matter explained why the natural motions of the heavens were not rectilinear, like those of the elements here on earth, but circular. The spheres rotate in different directions and at different speeds, but what is common to all of them is that they revolve around a centre.

While this depiction of the universe may strike us as fanciful, in our post-Copernican world and with our instruments and knowledge, it seemed at the time to be a reasonable attempt at making sense of the way the skies appeared from our vantage point here on earth. Maimonides did not doubt the entire physical picture that was generally accepted at the time, but he questioned its explanatory power. Astronomers can describe what they see, but cannot explain why the heavenly bodies move the way that they do. 'For his purpose is not to tell us in which way the spheres truly are, but to posit an astronomical system in which it would be possible for the motions to be circular and uniform and to correspond to what is apprehended through sight, regardless of whether or not things are thus in fact' (2:24, 326). By contrast with events here on earth, we do not have access to the causes of the heavenly motions, so 'regarding all that is in the heavens, man grasps nothing but a small measure of what is mathematical' (2:24, 326). The moon's sphere is that which immediately surrounds Earth, and is the boundary between the subject matter of sublunar physics, which can be understood properly, and that of celestial physics, regarding which Aristotle's teachings are, 'except for certain things, something analogous to guessing and conjecturing' (2:22, 320).

A couple of examples of Maimonides' difficulties with the Aristotelian picture will suffice here. For example, Aristotle taught that motion derives from the outermost sphere, which rotates from East to West. Other spheres move from West to East. Maimonides argues that were Aristotle's principles to be followed, the heavens ought to behave uniformly and mechanically, but they do not. Not only do their directions differ, but their speed too. 'Then there is the fact that one sphere is relatively slower, while another is more rapid; and this, as you know, does not correspond to the relations obtaining between the distances of the various spheres from each other' (2:19, 311). If the superlunar realm followed the rules that hold beneath the moon, there would be no reason for a sphere to move faster than the one above it. If anything, it ought to move more slowly. Nevertheless, from what can be witnessed, it appears as though this is a phenomenon that does in fact take place. Further evidence appears in the motions that seem not to follow an explicable pattern. Aristotle explained that circular motion takes place around a fixed midpoint, which ought to be the earth but, in order to make sense of what appears to the naked eye, different midpoints must be posited for different spheres. We also see that some of the planets seem to move backwards on occasions, and this too makes little sense from the perspective of Aristotelian physics.

In short, the only way to make sense of the superlunar motions is to posit ideas that are 'entirely outside the bounds of reasoning and opposed to all that has been made clear in natural science' (2:24, 322). However, all of these features can be accounted for if, rather than being natural, they are the result of a purposive intention, an activity aimed at creating them as they are. Of course, since Maimonides also professes a good deal of ignorance of the heavens, this evidence is not certain. However, since it appears that there is some cause particularising the heavens, as they do not follow an obvious natural pattern, Maimonides argues that they indicate a creator who is able to particularise generally. If this is the case, it can count as support for the view that the creator is able to particularise matters in the sub-lunar realm as well. And, if so, it counts as support for the Law's doctrines as a whole, including origination. Maimonides admits that the astronomical evidence is not certain, and that it may simply reflect a lack of understanding: 'It is possible that someone else may find a demonstration by means of which the true reality of what is obscure for me will become clear to him'

(2:24, 327). It is nevertheless sufficiently acceptable to support his argument, given the limitations he draws around what humans can know and the impossibility of depicting origination.

To sum up, Maimonides does not adopt the reasoning of those who argue that one of the alternatives is impossible. Nor does he ultimately argue that either is physically possible. Instead, he argues that there is no way of knowing whether or not creation is possible. We do not know that it is impossible for God. There is no definite reason to think that it is and, if God is to be a voluntary agent, it must be possible. We cannot know that God is a voluntary agent, but we do know that many of the Law's teachings depend on it being the case that God is, and both the Law and astronomical observations provide evidence that ought to be taken into account. Both indicate that the world is particularised and therefore created through purpose. Although, as seen in Chapter 3, the divine intention is not knowable to us, the evidence for particularisation indicates that God does indeed create with such purpose. Particularisation in the sublunar world allows for miracles and requires God to be able to cause material beings to be otherwise than they are. It is therefore connected with the belief that God causes matter, the individuating principle. While material beings are not subject to human knowledge, the Law teaches that they are not beyond God's causative knowledge. We can see here how Maimonides regards the Law's interconnected teachings as dialectical evidence that can be used to argue in favour of the position that would enable them, creation *ex nihilo* and *de novo*.

The issue discussed in this chapter has for decades been one of the most contested aspects of Maimonides' thought. One of the ways in which scholarly discussion of Maimonides is unusual, by comparison with other medieval philosophers, is that the debate often revolves not around what his arguments mean but, instead, whether he really believed them to be solid. Rather than focusing on the arguments about creation, a good deal of the scholarship asks which of the three opinions, Plato, Aristotle, or the Law, represent Maimonides' real view. Why might someone think that Maimonides hoped that an educated and perceptive reader would detect that he is hiding his view? Broadly, reasons can be divided into two kinds, external to the *Guide* or to Maimonides' corpus as a whole, or internal to Maimonides' text.

By external reasons to claim that Maimonides hides his opinion, I mean assumptions or opinions about philosophers or the history of philosophy that a reader brings to bear on her interpretation. Many assert that there is a fundamental incompatibility between religion and philosophy and claim that philosophers throughout history have shared such a view. However, they could not always express such an opinion openly. Reasons for their hesitance would have been either self-preservative or for the protection of those who are not philosophers, i.e., to avoid damaging their faith. In the present case, this is applied to the claim that philosophy taught that the world is everlasting and religion taught that it is not. It is then often thought that, as a philosopher, Maimonides would have understood that the world is everlasting but, as an adherent of a religious tradition that teaches otherwise, he would have publicly argued against such a view.

In order to argue that an author did not believe his or her own explicit claims, someone would have to present good reasons. For example, one could point out that the view in question was forbidden by certain authorities or that it would have been dangerous for an author to write it in public. However, there were Muslim and Jewish thinkers who openly espoused an eternal creation without dire consequences. Explaining creation in such a manner is not something that would obviously have led to Maimonides being persecuted. In his earlier writing, he did not even insist on creation *de novo* at all. While it is true that he did not flesh out what he meant by creation until writing the *Guide*, the *Code* and the early version of his Mishnah commentary are both open to an eternal creation and may even be easier to interpret in that way. As far as is known, this caused him no problems. Controversies followed his *Code*, but they did not concern anything he did or did not say about creation. Moreover, there is no reason that this particular evidence should apply specifically to a doctrine of creation. If Maimonides did not wish to disclose his opinions for fear of persecution, there are other doctrines that might seem to place him in greater danger, and his response to evil seems far more opposed to a stereotypical religious faith than a belief in eternal creation would be. Any response to such claims will therefore benefit from a more comprehensive approach that addresses the way in which Maimonides presents his arguments as a whole.

But, even should a reader reject these claims, or believe them not to be relevant to all philosophers, the external reasons appear to be supported, in the case of Maimonides, by internal reasons. What I mean by reasons internal to the text are literary signs or devices that indicate that the author is not writing in a straightforward fashion. One could argue that an author is writing with a degree of irony, and would expect his readers to understand when he is sending something up. Communication is not always direct, and it is certainly not always direct in the *Guide*. It is not written to be read as if it were a straightforward work of philosophy. In our case, justifications have been historical, literary and philosophical. The fact they have taken so many different forms indicates that there is a powerful case for seeking a hidden opinion, so it is a claim that demands a response. I will return to these issues in the concluding chapter. For now, I will simply mention that I think that there are more persuasive reasons to accept that Maimonides was sincere in his arguments for creation.

5

The Nature of Belief in God's Existence

There are a number of doctrines Maimonides considers fundamental to monotheism, and therefore to Judaism, that he argues
can be demonstrated. These are God's existence, unity, and incorporeality, and he refers to them as 'the three great and sublime
problems' (1:71, 181). A 'problem' is something that is offered up for
discussion, the point being that they are matters to be investigated
and proven rather than that they present problems for a believer.
Maimonides is uncompromising on all three of these. Many other
theologians were equally sure that God is an incorporeal unity, so
this insistence does not set him apart so much, and Maimonides'
general approach to these three issues is not controversial, or even
particularly unusual. However, the same cannot be said about
some of the ramifications he draws, particularly regarding how we
can or cannot use words to refer to God. His treatment of the three
'great and sublime' issues underpins both his arguments that God
has no attributes and his ensuing negative theology, something for
which he is usually, depending on the reader, either celebrated or
notorious. His so-called doctrine of negative attributes is one of
the philosophical teachings for which he is best known, and he
has a reputation for having taken a particularly hard line. In the
Latin world, Maimonides became known as an extreme proponent
of negative theology in the wake of Aquinas' critique, and some
philosophers writing in Hebrew also took issue with him. In my
view, Maimonides is not as negative as he is today often thought
to be. The disagreement that later thinkers have concerns the way
that we can use words rather than what can be known about God.

Many of his medieval critics advance theories that are grounded in the same idea that informs Maimonides' arguments, a doctrine of divine simplicity. Understanding that God is an absolute unity, simple in the sense of being completely indivisible, is essential to a true monotheistic belief. Any defect in belief in God's oneness is, in Maimonides' view, tantamount to idolatry and believing in divine simplicity involves understanding what it means to say that God is the Necessary Existent. Explaining Maimonides' negative theology should therefore be prefaced by what Maimonides says about God's existence. This chapter covers his arguments for God's existence and unity, and explains what Maimonides means by saying that they must be believed and known. Chapter 6 will address whether there is any way to understand what it might mean to say that God is the Necessary Existent and whether words can be used of such a being.

To appreciate the significance of saying that God's existence, incorporeality, and unity are demonstrable, let's revisit the distinction between demonstration and dialectic. Chapter 4 explained that Maimonides' arguments for creation are dialectical in nature, and that one of the reasons he employed dialectic is that creation is a realm in which there can be no certainty. He argues that it is impossible to conceive creation, let alone to be sure that it did or did not take place. Arguments either for or against either position can only be dialectical, based on premises that are generally accepted or taken from trusted sources, and can only try to show that one of the alternatives is more likely than the other. One can believe that the world had an absolute beginning or that it did not, but there is no way to be certain of that belief. By contrast, Maimonides claims certainty for the beliefs that God exists, is an absolute unity, and is incorporeal. The upshot is that these are matters that he thinks can be known, not merely believed, because they can be proven.

These ideas are so fundamental to Maimonides' conception of Judaism that he includes them among the legal obligations that the halakha imposes. The rabbinic tradition distinguishes between commandments held to be present in the Pentateuch, the written Torah, and others, including those derived by the rabbis through a set of norms mandated by the written Torah, which is believed to have been revealed to Moses at Sinai. The latter set of commandments is part of the oral Torah, a teaching that can encompass the entire tradition of Jewish thought developed since the Sinaitic revelation, whereas the former is held to have been given to Moses during that revelation. There are said to be 613 commandments in the first five biblical books. Scholars began to list them during the Geonic era, which is usually dated from the end of the sixth century to around the middle of the eleventh. Maimonides' *Book of Commandments* was his contribution to this genre, motivated by his dissatisfaction with his predecessors' lists. This work, written in Arabic, begins with the command to believe that God exists. It is followed by the command to affirm God's unity and another commandment, to love God. Loving God involves understanding creation, and understanding leads to true pleasure, which is a point I explained in Chapter 2. In Herbert Davidson's words, Maimonides thought that 'knowledge is the foundation on which the entire Jewish religion rests'.[1] Knowledge characterises both the beginning and the end of the *Code*, which starts with these three command-ments and finishes with a depiction of the messianic era, portrayed by Maimonides as a time of peace pervaded by love of knowledge. Knowledge is a motivating human drive, and knowledge of God is the goal. But knowledge of God is not, in itself, the initial drive, since the desire to know something requires a prior recognition that there is something there to be known, so knowing God is a command addressed to everyone. Nevertheless, not everyone can fulfil the command in the best possible way, at least not at first. Of course, relatively few understand the proofs, and those who do not must be taught to accept on the basis of 'traditional authority' that God is one and incorporeal (1:35, 81). But at this early stage they do not adequately believe these claims to be true, the reason being that they believe through what was known as 'imitation', which I will come to below, and do not understand what the doctrines mean.

In the *Guide*, Maimonides explains that 'belief is not the notion that is uttered, but the notion that is conceived in the soul when it has been averred of it that it is in fact just as it has been conceived … belief is the affirmation that what has been represented is outside the mind just as it has been represented in the mind.' (1:50, 111). This statement appears at the beginning of the section on divine attributes. It is relevant that Maimonides introduces his account of God's attributes by stating the importance of reasoned belief for an adequate understanding of the doctrines he is about to discuss. He is talking about a kind of belief that is the result of acknowledging something to be true. Maimonides needs to stress proper belief at the beginning of this section in order to pre-empt those who profess belief in divine unity but, since they do not understand what it must entail, continue to attribute to God words that are incompatible with such unity. He begins in this way because it is important to recognise that real belief in divine simplicity involves understanding what exactly is assented to. Here, he echoes an idea that appears in classical Islamic theology, in which true religious belief is considered to be a cognitive judgement. A true believer is someone who knows and understands the concepts assented to, not someone who simply believes on the authority of a tradition or of teachers. Genuine belief requires a mental assertion. Since Maimonides presents it as fundamentally cognitive in nature, one might conclude that he is making the apparently strange claim that belief and knowledge are identical. But it is not quite exact to say that Maimonides is using 'belief' in the *Guide* as a simple synonym for 'knowledge'. Indeed, the same word appears only a few chapters later in connection with people who believe something that is false, that the creator has attributes (1:53, 119). Here too, a judgement is involved. Even so, because of Maimonides' account of belief, and also because he himself seems to translate 'belief' as 'knowledge', the term has been the source of some confusion. The evidence that Maimonides translates belief as knowledge can be taken from comparing the *Book of Commandments* to the way he explains the commandment in the *Code*, which begins with the following parallel command to the obligation to believe found in the Arabic list: 'the basic principle of all basic principles and the pillar of all sciences is to know that there is a prime existent who brought every existing thing into existence'. Notice that the commandment in the *Code*, which is in Hebrew, is 'to know'. In contrast, in the *Book of Commandments*, Maimonides uses the same Arabic term for belief as he uses in the *Guide* (i'tiqād). It seems, then, that Maimonides' own translation of the term indicates that he equates knowledge with belief.

However, the important point in this comparison is not that belief means knowledge. In this particular case, because Maimonides thinks that God's existence can be proven, a command to believe and understand the proofs will be the same as a command to know, but a command to believe and understand a view for which there is no proof would not also be a command to know. Rather than attempting to identify knowledge and belief, then, Maimonides is here drawing on the idea that there are different levels of belief, each of which involves a judgement that something is or is not the case. For example, I can believe that the entire universe is made up of quarks even if I do not understand the physics that prove it to be true. I can even parrot the claim that there are quarks, and believe that they exist, without any real understanding of what quarks are supposed to be. But that would be an inferior form of belief. To believe in the fullest sense that the universe is made up of quarks, I would need to understand the evidence proving it to be true. An example with which Maimonides was familiar would be a belief that the world is spherical. Through a series of physical and astronomical arguments, Aristotle and Ptolemy showed that the world is a sphere. Someone in Maimonides' time could have accepted that the world is round, and could even have felt utterly convinced that it is true, simply because they had always been told that the world is round. But without understanding the proofs that the scientists advanced, they would not have a genuinely thought-through belief. Instead, they would believe through 'imitation', which involves copying beliefs of respected figures like teachers or leaders. However, in order to believe in the fullest sense in these doctrines, imitation is not enough, as it is an inferior form of belief.

Imitation is also unreliable. A deficient kind of belief that merely accepts something on the basis of someone else's say so, rather than reason's authority, would be vulnerable for two reasons. Firstly, there is the simple problem that it would be easy to convince someone of the opposite belief, if they have no firm basis for their opinion. If someone holds a true belief but does not understand why it is true, they would be unable to defend that belief from critique, even if the criticisms can be answered. Somebody who can defend the belief is on safer ground. Secondly, and importantly for Maimonides' chapter, the belief could still be scientifically questionable. In the case of a round earth, someone ignorant of the evidence could believe both that the earth is spherical and that it resides at the lowest point of the universe, topped by a dome in which the stars are fixed. There is nothing obviously wrong with positing that the two beliefs are compatible. Someone who does not understand those demonstrations for the earth's sphericity that are based on the movement and positions of the stars would not know that the proofs show that the earth is not at the bottom of a dome. It is therefore important to have good reasons for believing something.

In line with Muslim theologians,[2] Maimonides holds that this idea can also be applied to belief in God, both in God's existence and God's simplicity. Again, Maimonides states that everybody, no matter their intellectual level and training, should be taught to believe, on the basis of imitation, that God exists and that God is one. Nevertheless, to believe properly in God's unity requires understanding what it means to say that God is one. Those who believe without understanding could easily make a similar mistake to that explained above about the world being round. They could say that God is one but believe that God has attributes. In this case, they do not really believe in divine unity even though they pay lip service to it: 'if, however, someone believes that He is one, but possesses a certain number of essential attributes, he says in his words that He is one, but believes Him in his thought to be many' (1:50, 111). Such a statement resembles Christian doctrine, says Maimonides. If he was aware of any sophisticated Christian theology, there is no indication that he felt the need to write about it, or to consider it in depth. Here, he simply takes for granted that the doctrine of the Trinity is incoherent, and he likens it to the claim that God is one but has essential attributes. Since true belief in divine unity requires understanding why it must be said that God is one, Maimonides says that someone who holds an adequate belief would understand that it is incompatible with affirming that God has essential attributes. But, given that there are people who purport to believe both, he needs to address their claims. What they profess is similar to asserting a belief in a square circle; a logical impossibility that, as I mentioned in Chapter 4, is something that cannot even be conceived. 'In accordance with this, you will find many stupid people holding to beliefs to which, in their representation, they do not attach any meaning whatever' (1:50, 111). They do not assert anything in which it is possible to believe, but simply mouth words. Someone who believes that God has attributes believes in something fictional, says Maimonides, and 'has abolished his belief in the existence of the deity without being aware of it' (1:60, 145). It is important to understand what is implied by a doctrine of divine unity because you can only grasp its meaning and ramifications if you do so.

Given the point Maimonides is making, he is justified in expressing the Arabic term with the Hebrew for 'to know'. For one thing, 'belief' (*emuna*) sounds closer to an alternative Arabic word (*īmān*). Moreover, if the command is not only to believe, but also to understand that belief, there is no problem in Maimonides using both terms. Since both God's existence and uniqueness can be proven and, in principle, these proofs can be understood by anybody, the command to believe in them is simultaneously a command to know them. In this particular case, because the belief can be proven, reasoned belief results in knowledge. In Maimonides' presentation, the obligation is to understand the proofs for God's existence. The second commandment that he explains is to know that God is a unity. Again, this is something that he argues can be demonstrated to be true and we are commanded to know the proofs so as to understand, as far as possible, what it means to say that God is one. In the case of these demonstrable matters, then, true belief is knowledge. In contrast, someone who believes on the basis of imitation does not properly fulfil the commandment because they do not believe in the best way. Maimonides appears to emphasise the point when he demands from his readers to seek 'certain knowledge', which he describes as follows: 'if, together with this belief, one realises that a belief different from it is in no way possible and that no starting point can be found in the mind for a rejection of this belief or for the supposition that a different belief is possible, there is certainty' (1:50, 111).

Certainty characterises the most perfect form of scientific knowledge. Al-Fārābī explains the point in far more detail in some of his books on logic, using terms that Maimonides seems to allude to in this passage.[3] Propositions that can contain this kind of certitude, which al-Fārābī dubs necessary certitude, are universal propositions of the sort that can be used in scientific investigation. The highest level of certainty comes from a universal judgment that cannot be false. For example, there is certainty that what belongs to a human belongs to an animal. It cannot be otherwise because all humans are animals. What belongs to an animal might not belong to a human, however, since there are animals that have characteristics that humans do not. Al-Fārābī recognises different levels of certainty. Maimonides is simply summarising the idea and would, as usual, expect his ideal readers to be aware of such works as al-Fārābī's and to have studied them. It is important to note that certainty can also be a result of the process of acquiring knowledge. Properly understanding demonstrations leads to a sense of certainty. In such cases, it is necessary to know that an assertion is true, not simply to believe through imitation, for the demonstration provides the foundation of true scientific beliefs. These comments about belief and certainty connect Maimonides' discussion of divine attributes to the Arabic logical and epistemological tradition. He is concerned with how words can be used of God, so discussion of God's attributes must be scientifically rigorous and rest on a sound logical base if it is to avoid associating God with something non-divine, thereby making errors that are idolatrous.

Since Maimonides argues that proper belief in God involves knowing that there is a God, and since he argues that God's existence can indeed be demonstrated, another problem now arises. The problem is generated by the negative theology that he says follows from belief in divine simplicity. I will return to what negative theology amounts to in Chapter 6. For now, keep in mind simply that Maimonides argues that all attributes must be denied of God, and that these attributes include definitions. God cannot be defined, he says, so shouldn't it follow that God cannot be proven? In any proof, the first step ought to be defining the terms used. It would seem, then, that there cannot be any demonstration of God's existence, for any that Maimonides offers will fail to fulfil one of the basic conditions of a demonstration, that it is clear what the demonstration is about. You can't prove that something exists if you don't know what it is you are trying to prove. Nevertheless, Maimonides argues that it is possible to prove that the world as a whole cannot be self-sufficient, and that it therefore requires a cause, even if that cause is so different to any created cause that the cause cannot properly be understood. The claim that anything that can be proven to exist would automatically be a knowable object of reason is widespread in modern thought. Since Kant, many logicians assume that all demonstrations must involve terms that are properly defined and fully understood. Not all medieval thinkers agreed. They distinguished between an 'absolute demonstration' and a 'demonstration if', demonstrations that became known in Latin as *propter quid* and *quia*.[4] The former demonstrates that something is the case and also explains why it is; the latter only proves that it is. Maimonides' proofs are 'demonstrations if', and they are designed to prove 'that' God exists but not 'why' God exists: they show that God is but not what God is. In his view, there is no need to conclude that God must be limited to an object of human reason in order for his arguments to be accepted. Aristotle offers a couple of examples to explain the difference between an argument that proves a fact and an argument that explains the fact. One is taken from the fact that the moon waxes. Consider the following syllogism: that which waxes is spherical; the moon waxes; therefore, the moon is spherical. Here, the argument shows that the moon is spherical but not why it is spherical. Perhaps its waxing explains how we know that it is spherical, but it does not explain its very sphericity. Let's change the propositions around: that which waxes is spherical; the moon is spherical; therefore, the moon waxes. In this case, the argument explains why the moon waxes: it does so because it is spherical. Aristotle explains that the difference lies in the fact that 'it is not because of its waxing that the moon is spherical: rather, because it is spherical it waxes in this way'.[5] Similarly, arguments for God's existence are supposed to show that God exists, not to explain why God exists. Maimonides' proofs therefore proceed from facts about the world and try to account for the phenomena, arguing that they must be caused, rather than presenting a scientific explanation explaining fully why they are caused, i.e., what the motivation of the cause is. If Aristotle's statement were to be applied to these arguments, it would explain that 'it is not because the world exists that God causes it; rather, it is because God causes the world that it exists'. The arguments are not designed to show why the world is created, only that it is so. In that case, while Kant argued that rationally proving something's existence reduces that thing to an object of reason, Maimonides and others could disagree, since they thought that a demonstration can show that something exists even if that thing is not explained. Returning to al-Fārābī's account of certainty, al-Fārābī argues that a demonstration of the reasoned fact is most properly considered certain, as it combines both aspects, proving both the fact and its explanation. However, he grants that it is possible to gain certain knowledge that a thing exists even without knowing its cause. This latter type is the sort of demonstration that Maimonides employs to prove God's existence.

It is almost time to move onto the arguments for God's existence and unity themselves but, first, a few words about where Maimonides places them is appropriate because they do not appear until deep into the *Guide*. Maimonides presents these proofs only at the beginning of part two, a position that seems puzzling and would not make much sense if the *Guide* were an ordinary philosophical work, since a good deal of the points he makes in the first part depend on them. That is, throughout the first part, the reader must simply assume that God exists and is an incorporeal unity because that idea grounds the biblical interpretations that make up much of the first part. It is also the basis of the chapters expressly dedicated to denying that a simple God can have attributes, but the proofs for these doctrines only arrive later on. However, there is good reason that Maimonides organises the book in such a way. Recall that it is addressed to a particular student, Joseph ben Judah, whom Maimonides taught in person but who had left Egypt. It opens with a letter in which he writes that he is addressing Joseph and others like him. Maimonides mentions that he began to reveal 'the secrets of the prophetic books' to Joseph after they had studied the preparatory sciences together. The early chapters of the *Guide* therefore deal with exactly those secrets. Since much of Maimonides' exegesis involves explaining terms that would indicate that God has attributes, if they are taken literally, it makes sense for the question of divine attributes to arise during the course of this first part. In the letter to Joseph, after relating that he had begun to explain the deeper meanings, Maimonides writes, 'you demanded of me additional knowledge and asked me to make clear to you certain things pertaining to divine matters, to inform you of the intentions of the Mutakallimūn in this respect, and to let you know whether their methods were demonstrative and, if not, to what art they belonged' (1, Epistle Dedicatory, 4). The *Guide* is, in part, a response to this request. Maimonides reaches his summary of the kalām doctrines only at the end of the first part, after several reminders that it is important to study in the correct order, and after many chapters relating to the proper meaning of scriptural terms and passages that require interpretation, as well as chapters relating to the divine attributes, which are an integral part of this exegesis. When elaborating on the kalām arguments, he explains their approach to the 'three problems', God's existence, unity, and incorporeality, and also to creation. Together, he refers to them as 'four problems'. The end of part one therefore leads into part two, in which Maimonides explains what he takes to be the correct approach to these questions. When introducing his account of the kalām, he therefore writes as follows:

> I shall mention the premises of the Mutakallimūn and shall make clear their methods by means of which they elucidate the four problems in question. After that I shall set down for your benefit other chapters in which I shall make clear to you the premises of the philosophers and their methods of inference with regard to these problems. (1, 71, 183)

In the *Guide's* first part, the structure follows the order in which Maimonides presents the issues in the letter, and it makes good sense in light of the didactic scheme he adopts. Maimonides explains biblical terms that appear to indicate that God is physical and, therefore, lead to 'perplexity'. He then addresses the requests that Joseph made when asking for instruction in 'divine matters' and guidance regarding kalām methodology. Joseph asked whether their methods are demonstrative. Maimonides outlines their opinions and criticises their arguments, which are rhetorical and dialectical. At the end of the first part, then, Maimonides arrives at his response to Joseph's request. It is reasonable for him to follow his summary of the kalām's arguments for the four issues with his own. We need to recognise that there are bad arguments for the four issues at stake, but there are good ones too, so Maimonides will need to explain them as well. As part of the *Guide's* overall structure, it is fitting that the proofs for God's existence and unity appear after the account of divine attributes. There is no need to follow Maimonides' order of presentation here, though, and I will now jump forward to the demonstrations in the *Guide's* second part before returning in Chapter 6 to the consequences for religious language that he derives from them.

In order to prepare the ground for these arguments about God's existence, Maimonides begins the second part by summarising 25 scientific positions that he says have been demonstrated by the philosophers. As usual, he does not outline or defend the demonstrations, or even explain all of the points in detail. Instead, he expects those readers who can understand the scientific discussions adequately to be able to access the books that prove them. These 25 theses could be considered a synopsis of Aristotelian science, and they serve as premises for his arguments. However, Maimonides adds another premise, which he says has not been demonstrated but is nevertheless crucial for the sake of these demonstrations, the eternity of the world.

If Maimonides grants for the sake of his arguments that the world is eternal, and also claims that it has to be accepted in order to demonstrate that God exists, does this mean that he must himself accept that the world is eternal? If someone is to deny that the world is eternal, would that undermine the demonstrations? Furthermore, if God's existence is demonstrated, shouldn't that mean that the premises used to prove it are true and, moreover, certain? I mentioned in Chapter 4 that many do indeed claim that Maimonides believed the world to be eternal. His arguments for God's existence do not count as evidence in that context though. Bear in mind that the debate over the world's eternity is not the question he is addressing here. Instead, he is offering proofs for God's existence, which are also proofs for God's unity and incorporeality. He therefore supplements the proofs that employ the premise of eternity with the following argument. Either the world is eternal or it is not. If the world is eternal, God exists. If the world is not eternal, God exists. Therefore, God exists. Maimonides must follow this line of reasoning because one of the criticisms he levelled against kalām arguments is that they assume what they are trying to prove (1:71, 178). Since the premise itself is uncertain, no proof based on only one of the alternatives can be demonstrative, for the premise could be false. However, since the dichotomy is exhaustive, covering all possibilities, if God's existence can be shown to follow from both alternatives, it can be considered demonstrated. Maimonides claims that if the world did have a beginning, there is no need for an argument to show that there must be a creator, since there must be an explanation as to why it came into being in the first place. 'This is a first intelligible, for everything that exists after having been nonexistent must have of necessity someone who has brought it into existence – it being absurd that it should bring itself into existence' (2:2, 252). He therefore needs only to prove that God's existence follows also if the world did not have a beginning.

Maimonides enumerates four proofs for God's existence. These chapters at the beginning of part two make much of the number four, which Maimonides says 'should be an object of reflection' (2:10, 272). Aspects of Aristotelian science also involve quartets, and it is important for parts of Maimonides' biblical exegesis too, but I will not go into that here. Among the proofs, two begin from observing motion in the world and two from more fundamental ideas about the principles of existing things. The proofs themselves are somewhat technical, and appear to be of varying quality. I will explain only two of them here, the first and the third. They seem to be the strongest of the four. The proofs from motion depend on Aristotelian physics and can easily appear somewhat outdated. Proofs of the second kind might seem today to be more promising. Both are worth outlining in any case, since both kinds were widely used.

The first proof begins by observing that material things in our world are in motion and by recognising that they do not ultimately move themselves. Even living things, which have internal principles of motion, are motivated to move by something outside of themselves or to fulfil a need. They move in order to acquire something, like food or drink, or to flee from something, whether it is dangerous or simply disagreeable. As I explained in Chapter 2, Aristotle argued that things in our world would rest once they reach their natural positions so, since they are perpetually in motion, there must be something generating the motion, and he identified the cause as the motion of the heavens. All sublunar motion can be traced to the heavenly sphere's motion. Let's assume, in accord with the twenty-sixth premise, that the world's motion is eternal. That is, the motion of the heavens which is, in Aristotle's physics, responsible for the motion in the world, is eternal. Given that matter does not move itself, a material being needs something to move it, in order to receive form, and, since the sphere is material, it must be moved too. Where does this eternal motion come from?

To cover all the possibilities, Maimonides makes the following distinctions. The motion must either derive from something other than the sphere or from the sphere itself. If it is external to the sphere, the mover must either be a body or not. If it is from the sphere itself, the motive force must be divisible or indivisible. In total, then, there are four possibilities: two are general and each have two sub-possibilities. He lists them in the following order.

1. The sphere is moved by an external body.
2. The sphere is moved by an incorporeal force separate from it.
3. The sphere moves itself with a divisible force.
4. The sphere moves itself with an indivisible force.

Maimonides proceeds to eliminate the first, third, and fourth, leaving only the option that the mover is an incorporeal force that is not a part of the sphere. To see why he argues this, let's consider first what the rejected alternatives amount to and why he thinks them impossible.

The first possibility is that the sphere is moved by an external body. If this is the case, the external body itself would have to be in motion. Maimonides argues that a body can only move another body if the first is itself in motion. For example, a ball would only cause another ball to move if it is itself moving. The chain of motion itself must be set in motion by something else, a person, who is a self-mover. We are assuming for now that the sphere is not a self-mover, and the body that is posited to explain the motion cannot be a self-mover either, for those are the alternative positions Maimonides will dispense with afterwards. So, if the sphere's motion is caused by another body, that other body must be in motion. The same question arises about this second body: from where does its motion derive? It is always possible to posit another moving body as the motion's source, but adding bodies must at some point come to an end as there cannot be an infinite number of bodies existing together, says Maimonides in the second of the 25 premises: 'The existence of magnitudes of which the number is infinite is impossible – that is, if they exist together' (2: Introduction, 235). There are several arguments designed to show that an infinite bodily extension is impossible, and I mentioned the point in Chapter 4 as well. As is often the case, and as I have repeated several times, Maimonides himself does not explain the grounds underlying his statements, but they appear in books on physics that he expects readers to consult. One such argument, which I use because of its brevity, asks what would happen were a part of the infinite isolated from the rest. Presumably, the rest would still be infinite. If it is truly infinite, it would be unlimited, but that can no longer be the case since a limit has been drawn in order to separate the isolated part. The idea that body can be infinitely extended was therefore considered absurd. In that case, since body must be moved by something, and body cannot be infinite, the first option must be ruled out. The sphere's infinite motion cannot have an external body as its ultimate cause.

Now three alternatives remain, and the next to be rejected is the idea that the sphere is moved by an innate, divisible force pervading it entirely, the third of the four possibilities. As in the refutation of the first alternative, Maimonides states that body must be finite. The sphere is therefore finite and any force that it contains must also be finite. That a finite body cannot contain an infinite force is set out in premise twelve. Again, no argument is offered. A brief one pictures the body divided into separate parts and asks what would happen to the force. Would the force in each part be finite or infinite? If they are finite, they could not be combined to make up an infinite force, and if they are infinite, the force in a part would be identical to the force in the whole. This second option is considered absurd because a whole cannot be identical with a single one of its parts. Perhaps one part would be considered infinite while the rest remain finite, but that option would be subjected to the same criticism mentioned above when rejecting the first theory about motion's origin. Dividing a finite from an infinite would automatically limit the infinite and lead to absurdity. If the motion is caused by an innate, divisible force, it therefore cannot be caused by an infinite force and the motion cannot be infinite. Since we are trying to account for infinite motion, this alternative must also be ruled out.

Nor can the mover be an indivisible force internal to the sphere. This would be similar to the way in which a human soul moves the body – the soul is not divided if part of the body that it moves is: it remains in only one part of that body – and Maimonides says that this sort of force would also be incapable of causing infinite motion. He argues that this conclusion follows from observing that the mover would itself be moving, but only accidentally. If the mover is in the body, and the body is moving, it is clear that the mover is also in motion. When a person moves, the soul moves the body, and the soul's purpose is to move the person, not to move only the soul itself. Nevertheless, by virtue of the fact that it is located in the moving body, the soul moves as well. It causes the motion but is itself transported so, when the body stops moving, the soul also stops moving. The soul is therefore in motion only accidentally. Maimonides then introduces the premise that everything that is in motion accidentally must at some point come to rest. This premise puzzled some of the *Guide's* medieval commentators, since Avicenna held that the spheres had souls and also held that the sphere moves eternally. Therefore, the philosophers seem to hold that the spheres' souls could be moving accidentally and eternally. Given that Maimonides is supposed to be arguing on the basis of the philosophers' opinions, he ought not to be entitled to use the premise. However, the souls were not supposed to be the spheres' ultimate movers, and the point seems to be that the first mover, in particular, cannot be in motion accidentally, not that accidental motion generally cannot be eternally caused. The fact that it's not in the nature of the soul to be always in motion doesn't mean that it cannot constantly be moved, simply that it is not constantly in motion of its own accord. For instance, the soul is only in motion when the body is, so even were we to suppose that the body's motion is eternally caused by the soul, the very motion of the soul would depend on the body, and the soul's motion would need to be caused by something else. That cause cannot be the soul itself, because a soul moves its body in view of factors external to the ensouled body. An animal moves in order to achieve something, either to satisfy a desire or to avoid something disagreeable, or to reach a goal it sets for itself, or perhaps in order to expend excess energy. If none of these external factors is present, the animal does not move voluntarily. If the sphere's motion is ultimately caused by something like a soul, it therefore cannot be eternal because such a motion would require another cause motivating the soul. This fourth alternative is therefore also ruled out.

Having rejected three of the four alternative sources of motion, and asserted that one of the four must be true, Maimonides affirms the remaining option, that the sphere's motion is caused by an entity separate from the sphere itself. Since the mover is neither a body nor a force existing in a body, because these possibilities have been refuted, it cannot itself be in motion, as motion is a property of bodies. Neither can it be divided or changed. For this last pair

of denials, Maimonides invokes two more of the twenty-five philosophical premises. One might wonder whether he is putting these
premises to use incorrectly. The seventh includes the statement that
'everything that is indivisible is not movable; hence it will not be
a body at all' (2: Introduction, 235), but Maimonides uses it to say
that 'everything that is not a body is indivisible'. The fifth states
that 'every motion is a change and transition from potentiality to
actuality' (2: Introduction, 235), and he seems to use it in this proof
to say that 'every change is a motion'. In the case of the fifth, there
doesn't really seem to be a problem. The claim that all change is a
motion of some sort was uncontroversial in Aristotelian physics.
The seventh might pose more of a difficulty. Even if that which
is indivisible is not movable, because it is not a body, it does not
seem to follow that what is immovable is indivisible. Ideas and
essences are not movable in themselves, but they can be divided
mentally into such things as genus and species. Moreover, the
separate intelligences are immaterial and therefore immovable, but
they can be divided into essence and existence, a distinction I will
explain below because it is a crucial part of the proof from existence.
Maybe Maimonides' argument can be saved, since he only seems
to need to call on the idea that the cause is indivisible in the way
that bodies are indivisible. Once the sphere's motion is shown to
have been caused by a mover indivisible in such a way, the prime
mover has been demonstrated. There is a separate question about
the identity of the first mover, whether it is God or the first created
being, which Maimonides does not enter into here. Philosophers
disagreed on the matter – Alexander of Aphrodisias identified
them while Avicenna did not – and commentators on Maimonides
disagreed over what his opinion was. For the sake of this particular
proof, as he is presenting a proof from motion, he can suffice with
the conclusions of those who advocate such proofs. The prime
mover must exist and be an incorporeal unity. Here Maimonides'
first proof ends, and he writes, 'these are the three problems with
regard to which the most excellent among the philosophers gave
demonstrations' (2:1, 246).

A proof from motion could demonstrate the existence of a mover,
but Avicenna thought that such a mover need not also be the source
of the world's existence and is therefore not identical with God, the
Necessary Existent. He was dissatisfied with proofs from motion,
and tried to set God's existence on a firmer footing by beginning
from the general fact of existence instead. The argument that he
devised has been enormously influential and is still used in various

forms even today. Scholars have often noted that Maimonides' third demonstration bears some similarity to Avicenna's proof. Maimonides himself seems particularly convinced by the proof, stating that it 'is a demonstration concerning which there can be no doubt, no refutation, and no dispute, except on the part of one who is ignorant of the method of demonstration' (2:1, 248). Even though the argument is designed to show that God is the Necessary Existent, and therefore distinct from all created beings, both Avicenna and Maimonides agree that 'necessary existence' cannot be understood. It should not be taken as an explanation of God's true nature, but as a kind of placeholder that allows us to characterise the absolute difference between God's existence and that of everything else. God's nature cannot be known and neither can it be named in any simple sense. Despite the similarity between Maimonides' proof and that of Avicenna, they are not exactly the same. While Avicenna's argument is designed to stand whether or not the world is created *de novo*, Maimonides has already stated his commitment to using proofs based on the premise that it is not. Accordingly, Maimonides' version is in two parts, the first of which attempts to establish that there is a necessary existent, while the second elaborates on what that means. In the first part, he argues that there must be a necessary being and, in the second, he argues that the necessary being cannot be a part of the world. The second part is that in which Maimonides adopts Avicenna's language, although he presents it in an extremely truncated way that will require some explanation.

Maimonides begins by observing that sense perception shows that there are existing things. He argues that one of the following three statements must be true: none of them is subject to generation and corruption; all are subject to generation and corruption; some are subject to generation and corruption and some are not. He then rules out the first two, concluding that the third must be true. Sense evidence shows that objects come to be and pass away, so at least some of the existing things must be subject to generation and corruption. The question is whether all are. Maimonides now introduces a principle that sounds odd: 'it is indubitable, as you know, that what is possible with regard to a species must necessarily come about' (2:1, 247). This is a version of an idea known as the principle of plenitude and accords with Aristotle's division: what is always the case is necessary; what is sometimes the case is possible; what is never the case is impossible.[6] To illustrate the claim, consider the case of the blue buttercups. If it is genuinely possible that a buttercup be blue, it would at some point be true that a buttercup is blue. If no blue buttercup ever exists, it seems sensible to conclude that such a thing cannot take place. Or if no elephant ever grows wings, we can say that this is because it is not really possible for an elephant to do so. With this principle in mind, and given that these proofs are assuming the philosophers' claim that infinite time has already passed, Maimonides argues that all genuine possibilities would have already come about. Now if all existing things are contingent, and it is therefore genuinely possible for all of them to pass away, there would have been a time at which they had indeed all passed away. But this cannot have happened; had it done so, no things would exist now, since there would have been nothing to bring them into existence. However, 'we perceive things that are existent. In fact, we ourselves are existent' (2:1, 247). Therefore, there must be a being that is necessary and which cannot have passed away even in infinite time. The option, that some things are possible and at least one is necessary, is therefore the only one that is capable of accounting for the phenomena we see.

This is where the first part of Maimonides' proof ends. He cannot stop there though, if he is to assert that the Necessary Existent is necessary in the sense he requires, since the kind of necessity it argues for does not really capture his assertion that God's existence is necessary. It is reflected, however, in one of the ways that necessity is often explained today. Current philosophical discourse uses possible worlds ontology to explain what it means for something to be necessary. A possible world is a state of affairs that could be the case. There is a possible world in which I am not writing but, instead, playing football; there is another possible world in which I am a Hollywood actor, however unlikely that may seem. There is no possible world in which God does not exist because Maimonides holds that in order for anything at all to exist, God must exist. If there is no possible world in which God does not exist, it follows that it is necessary that God exists. However, while it is of great use, such a tool doesn't reflect what Maimonides means when he says that God is the Necessary Existent. It could be of help in explaining the issues in Chapter 4, regarding the necessity or otherwise of the world. If it is impossible for the world not to exist – if there is no possible world in which the world as a whole comes to be – the world's existence would be necessary. As that chapter explained, Maimonides recognises that such necessity cannot be ruled out with certainty. There can be no demonstration that the world is not a necessary corollary of God's existence, in which case it would exist always and would therefore be statistically necessary. However, even if the world were to be necessary in this sense, Maimonides would still insist that God's necessity is of a different kind. In the case of a necessary world that depends on God's eternal creative activity, the necessity would not be the defining feature of the world. It is therefore not applicable to the divine necessity, which, as I will explain in more detail in Chapter 6, Maimonides characterises as belonging to God alone in virtue of the claim that God's essence and existence are identical. A necessary being, in the sense that God must be necessary, is not merely statistically necessary but is *essentially* necessary.

Maimonides continues by reporting that the philosophers say that the being proved to be incorruptible must be necessary either through itself or through a cause. 'With reference to this existent's being necessary of existence, there are two possibilities: this may be either in respect to its own essence or in respect to the cause of this existent' (2:1, 248). He then explains that if this being is possible in itself, it must be caused, in which case its cause is necessary. Since a necessary being has already been argued for in the proof's first section, there must be a being that is not necessary only through something else, a cause, but is necessary in itself, and therefore uncaused.

In order to explain the distinction between something necessary in itself and something necessary through another, language that reflects Avicenna's argument, this part of the proof needs some explanation. Avicenna further clarifies the distinction between necessary, possible, and impossible: what is necessary must exist; what is possible can either exist or not exist; what is impossible cannot exist. Obviously, if things exist, they are not impossible, so each existing thing must be either possible or necessary. The claim that some existing beings are possible is grounded by a distinction between essence and existence. It is a distinction reflected in the fact that an answer to the question what something is differs from the answer to the question whether something is. For example, you can explain what a dinosaur or a dodo is without asserting that they still exist. A definition of these objects accounts only for what they are, and the definition is said to denote the essence of a thing. Since existence is not taken as part of the definition, there is no logical reason that these individuals should exist. They are 'possible of existence'. The same is true not only of dodos but also of individuals that exist now. I exist now, but I do not have to exist and someday will cease to do so. I will address the relationship between such objects and their existence in Chapter 6. For now, all that is required is for the distinction between essence and existence to be made. If it is legitimate, it follows that things do not explain their own existence and that they are contingent; in order to exist, they must be caused to do so by something external. When considered purely inasmuch as what they are, they might or might not exist.

While something 'possible' might or might not exist, what is 'necessary' must exist. However, Maimonides has distinguished something necessary in itself from something necessary through another, and what is necessary through another is, in itself, possible. A being necessary in itself is necessary through its own essence, and its existence is inherent. Denying it would therefore be asserting that there is something that lacks its own essence, like saying that a cow lacks bovine nature. If being bovine is what it is to be a cow, nothing can lack bovinity while being a cow. Similarly, no being that has necessity as part of its nature can be denied without self-contradiction. If its nature implies its existence, it cannot avoid existence as long as it has that nature. The same is not true of something that is necessary only through another. That thing is itself possible because existence is not essential to it and it depends on a cause in order to exist. However, once it has been caused to exist, its existence becomes necessary. Given the condition that it exists, it cannot also lack existence, for once a possibility has been actualised it is no longer merely possible. Take a seed, for example, which is potentially a tree and therefore has the possibility of growing into one. If it is planted somewhere with the right conditions, it will turn into a tree. After it has done so, it no longer has the mere possibility of becoming a tree. Now, because existence is divided into necessary and possible, and the tree is not simply possible, it must be necessary. Through the causes that activate it, the tree has become necessary. But since a tree's necessity is not essential to the tree, not being part of the tree's essence, it remains possible in itself and its necessity is derived from something else, through the causes that bring it about.

Since all individuals are only possible in themselves, we can ask why any one of them exists, and the reason will not be found in the individual itself. Instead, it is caused to exist by something else. No matter how many causes you posit, each individual will be caused. There is nothing obviously wrong with saying that there can be an endless succession of caused events, all of which come to be and pass away. Nevertheless, the entire succession will still be constituted of things possible in themselves each of which needs something else to make it exist. Is it possible for all things taken together to be contingent? That is, can the aggregate of contingent beings be self-sufficient, requiring no cause for its existence? Like Avicenna's argument, Maimonides' proof requires that it not be, that the aggregate, taken as a whole, would still not be self-explanatory. However, one could reasonably ask why the universe as a whole should be included among the possible things. It is difficult to make a case for the claim that the notion of possibility outlined here can be applied to the whole. The idea that beings are possible is based on distinguishing existence from essence. Now, while it seems simple enough to distinguish existence from individual essences, the universe as a whole doesn't have a definable essence. The universe isn't a thing that exists and can be defined: it just is the entirety of existence. Definitions classify things that are part of the world, not the entirety of existing things. It does not seem obvious that the distinction between essence and existence should apply to the aggregate of existing things. Furthermore, it might be tempting to charge Avicenna and Maimonides with an extremely basic fallacy, the fallacy of composition, which attributes what is true of all the parts of a whole to the whole itself. It is fallacious because there is no need for something to share the features that each of its parts has. For example, even if all players in a sports team have two legs, the team as a whole is not bipedal. The strategy therefore cannot be so simple as to apply the distinction between essence and existence to the aggregate of existing things without further justification.

Bear in mind that Avicenna argues that all existing things are either necessary through themselves or necessary through something else because, in order to exist, their causes must be present. He applies this distinction to the aggregate of all existing things, which is clearly something that exists, and asks whether this totality can be necessary through itself. If it can, there is no need to seek a further explanation that would cause it to exist since, if it is necessary, it must exist, for it contains the principle of its own existence. Avicenna argues that the aggregate cannot be necessary in itself because what is necessary in itself, and therefore exists in its own right, does not exist through something else. But the aggregate is made up of all its parts and something that is constituted of parts exists through those parts. A physical substance exists through matter and form, for instance, which are parts of the whole, and the substance depends on these parts. Similarly, the entire aggregate of existing things depends on its constituent parts. Therefore, if it is said to be necessary in itself, what is said to be necessary is in some sense dependent. However, to be necessary in itself is precisely to be not dependent, so to say that the aggregate is necessary would be self-contradictory. If the aggregate of existing things is necessary, then, it could only be so through something else. Now, if the aggregate is necessary through another, it is dependent on something that is itself necessary. The same question can be asked of whatever cause makes it necessary, no matter how many there may be. Avicenna can then conclude that the world is not necessary in itself and, given his explanation that things necessary through another require a cause, he concludes that the ultimate cause must be something necessary in itself. Without such a cause, nothing would have been brought about at all: there would not be any existent possible in itself but necessary through its causes.

Notice that the question is not whether or not there must have been something to kick off the entire chain of events. That would be a question of a different sort, and Avicenna expressly argues that even if the world is eternal, which he thinks it is, it would still not account for its own existence and would therefore require an external cause. If the attempt is to explain the aggregate, it cannot be an explanation of the same kind as one that would explain any of the individuals on their own. Even a remote and ultimate cause of the same kind would not be enough. If you were to posit a cause at the beginning of a chain, the cause could be considered a remote cause of everything that follows. Nonetheless, if it is still the same sort of cause, explaining in the same way as a familiar cause does, it would not be the cause that Avicenna seeks, for the cause would also require some sort of explanation. As Toby Mayer writes, 'the external cause of the aggregate of contingents cannot be contingent, on pain of dropping back within the very aggregate it has been adduced to explain'.[7] Asking what causes the aggregate is not like asking about any one of its parts. It is a unique question. Proofs of the sort that Avicenna advanced here are often understood to be getting at the strange question 'why is there anything rather than nothing?' Whatever answers that question would be the creator of everything but the answer must itself be mysterious: were it intelligible it would be part of what is being explained, and the question would be raised again. If the entirety of existence is contingent rather than necessary, it raises a question about its causes.

In light of these arguments, Maimonides has concluded that there must be a necessary existent and that, ultimately, there must be something that is necessary in itself. He then cites the argument that anything composite cannot be necessary and that, conversely, the Necessary Existent therefore cannot be composite but must, rather, be an absolutely simple unity, since anything with parts is dependent on those parts, and the Necessary Existent cannot be dependent. He also argues that something without composition cannot be instantiated more than once and that, therefore, there can be only one God. To see why, consider what must be true if there are multiple individuals of the same sort. Take, for example, Buddy and Rita, who are both dogs. They are different individuals with a common canine nature and this canine nature is what accounts for them being dogs. Their common nature differs from both of them: both are dogs but neither is caninity itself. Canine nature as a whole is different from the individual Buddy and the individual Rita. Let's say that this is not the case, that Buddy is not composite and is identical with his doggy nature. In that case, he is a dog inasmuch as he is Buddy. However, Rita cannot be a dog inasmuch as she is Buddy because she plainly is not Buddy. They can both share being dogs only if they themselves are distinct from what is shared. In that case, there must be a distinction between them and their nature, and they are composite. Since God is not composite, no such nature can be shared between God and anything else. God cannot be God inasmuch as God possesses some nature that could be shared with something else, since that would mean there is one thing that is God and another thing that is the nature through which God is God. Therefore, there can only be one God. As Maimonides writes, were there more than one, 'none of them would be necessary of existence in virtue only of itself, but it would be necessary of existence in virtue of the notion representing the species – necessity of existence – a species subsisting both in that particular being and in another one' (2:1, 248).

To finish this chapter, it is important to emphasise that Maimonides holds God's existence to be demonstrated even though he advances proofs employing a premise that is not, that the world is eternal. These proofs also demonstrate God's unity and incorporeality. However, while he says that God's existence is not in need of supporting arguments if the world is originated, he does not say the same about the other two claims, that God is simple and immaterial. These doctrines require further proofs, and Maimonides provides a number of them. Besides these extra proofs, he says that the third demonstration also shows these other two doctrines to be true even if the premise of an eternal world is rejected: 'the demonstration that He is one and not a body is valid, regardless of whether the world has come into being in time after having been nonexistent or not – as we have made clear by means of the third philosophic method' (2:2, 252). Maimonides seems to understand the section of the proof that he takes from Avicenna, divorced of the premise that the world is eternal, to be a demonstration of what must be true of a necessary being.[8] He seems to recognise that the second half of his own proof can stand independently of the first part as a proof of divine unity and incorporeality, even if he thinks the first part is needed in order to prove God's existence. If so, this would help his assertion that God's existence, unity, and incorporeality are all demonstrable even if creation itself is not.

6

Necessary Existence and Divine Attributes

If Maimonides claims to have demonstrated God's existence, you might expect him to say something about what God is like. Maimonides objects. We cannot know God's essence at all, he says, and the best way to speak about God is by using denials. This is at the root of much of the *Guide's* exegesis and is reflected in the first purpose that Maimonides assigns the work, to explain terms occurring in the Bible that need to be understood differently in different contexts. He explains that 'the Torah speaks in human language' (1:26, 56) in order to communicate with everyone, including those who have not studied at all. It therefore uses language that compares God to creatures and implies that God is physical. As I've emphasised numerous times, one of the *Guide's* stated aims is to explain terms that should not be taken literally but, in a chapter of the *Guide* that I'll address below (1:53), Maimonides explains that accepting the surface meaning led people to believe that God is physical. If that is the whole problem, Maimonides simply needs to explain that God is incorporeal, and that might seem a fairly simple task, since it is not very controversial today to deny that God is physical. Many in Maimonides' time, apparently including rabbinic authorities, believed that God has a body, although not necessarily one of flesh and blood, or can assume bodily form, so historical observations might therefore explain, to a certain degree, why Maimonides considered the issue to be so grave. However, his arguments are not merely historical curiosities. While it is probably fair to say that fewer Jews now consciously think that God has a body, Maimonides argues that beliefs common today imply God to be somehow physical. In his view, someone who believes that God deliberates or is affected by human actions in any way, whether that is by becoming angry or changing a thought to reward or punish, also believes that God is subject to material trappings. He argues that plenty of people believe that God has attributes and, even if such believers don't realise it, these attributes imply that God is material. Predicating any attribute at all of God compromises belief in God.

> I shall not say that he who affirms that God, may He be exalted, has positive attributes either falls short of apprehending Him or is an associator or has an apprehension of Him that is different from what He really is, but I shall say that he has abolished his belief in the existence of the deity without being aware of it. (1:60, 145)

Even saying that God has 'wisdom' or 'goodness' therefore violates the commandment to affirm God's unity. This leaves us with a difficulty, because there are times when Maimonides does indeed talk about God's wisdom, will, and knowledge. As usual, in order to appreciate what he is getting at, we need to pay attention to the context and rhetorical purpose of his arguments, and also to the qualifications he makes. Moreover, we will have to pay attention to what Maimonides says he means by 'attribute'.

Maimonides argues that although we can know that God exists and is a necessary unity, we cannot know God's essence: 'we are only able to apprehend the fact that He is and cannot apprehend His quiddity' (1:58, 135). The kind of knowledge that we have is necessarily limited, since it is only knowledge that there is such a being, which differs from the kind of understanding you have when you can properly define something by assigning it genus and species. Even though Maimonides claims that you cannot say exactly what God is, he has quite a lot to say about what God is not. The most appropriate way to speak about God, he says, is by negations, by denying that God has attributes, and the more attributes you deny, the better. Ultimately, all attributes need to be negated. For this reason, his is often considered a model example of negative theology. Indeed, he is sometimes considered to advocate an extreme version in which God is so removed from our thoughts or understanding as to be denied altogether.

Maimonides does indeed say that God's essence is unknowable and that God is most properly spoken of only through negations or attributes of action. However, this does not tell the whole story. The reason that, in Maimonides' view, language cannot capture God's essence is not that there is no God. Rather, language fails because God is the fullness of being, whose existence is entirely unlimited and contains no deficiencies or potentialities. Maimonides states that, unlike in created beings, there can be no distinction between essence and existence in a necessary being. This is his doctrine of divine simplicity, and it lies behind his negative theology. He argues that once the doctrine is properly understood, it becomes clear that God is indivisible and possesses no attributes. The third demonstration of God's existence, which was outlined at the end of Chapter 5, finishes with a statement of the doctrine that grounds his theology.

> Now it has been made clear in a number of ways that no duality at all, nor the existence of an equal or of a contrary, can be true with reference to the necessary of existence. The cause of all this is the latter's absolute simplicity and absolute perfection leaving no residue outside its essence that pertains to the species, the necessary of existence – as well as the nonexistence in any way of a primary or secondary cause for it. Accordingly, nothing at all can be associated with the necessary of existence. (2:1, 248–9)

Proofs that God is the Necessary Existent underlie all that Maimonides says about divine attributes. This chapter will outline Maimonides' so-called doctrine of negative attributes and therefore will also need to consider divine simplicity, which is expressed in the belief that God's existence is necessary. Since simplicity functions for Maimonides as a controlling notion for negative theology, there should be a way to elaborate on what we can understand by it. But divine simplicity has been subject to a number of critiques and misrepresentations in recent philosophy. This chapter is therefore divided into two sections. The first presents negative theology and the second offers an account of divine simplicity. Inevitably, I need to present some of the issues in an abbreviated way. Readers who wish to delve into the debate are advised to consult the items in the reading list at the end of this book. I am drawing on these discussions, and particularly on work by philosophers who are concerned to argue that God exists.[1] However, I do not here argue that there is or is not a simple God. Instead, my purpose is to give some idea of how Maimonides can be understood in a way that is intelligible in the context of current philosophical debates. Those who wish to leave out the more metaphysical analyses may skip over the second part.

1. Negative Theology: The Question of Divine Attributes

Let's return to the issue with which Maimonides begins this part on divine attributes, the nature of belief and a call to understand. He argues that once the doctrine of divine simplicity is properly understood, it becomes clear that God is indivisible and possesses no attributes. The *Guide*'s following chapters, from 51 to 60, draw out the consequences that Maimonides thinks follows. Since he began by criticising people who claim to believe in God's unity but do not, because they do not understand what the doctrine amounts to, and his general purpose in these chapters is to explain that divine unity is incompatible with the belief that God has attributes, he continues by objecting to the views that are inconsistent with simplicity. I mentioned in Chapter 5 that the way in which Maimonides arranges the *Guide* by placing proofs for God's simplicity after these chapters on negative theology makes sense from a didactic point of view, given his aim of explaining scripture and responding to his student's requests. The internal structure of these particular chapters on divine attributes also has a certain logic. One of the major thrusts of all the chapters leading up to these is to explain the deeper meanings of terms used of God in the Bible. Any words that are used of things that are composite or changing must be interpreted as metaphors, not literally. Maimonides now explains that such interpretation is needed because the doctrine of divine unity is incompatible with belief in a God that is divisible or changes. This is why, in chapter 50, he explains that real belief requires understanding.

Chapter 51 continues with the same theme, explaining that it ought to be obvious that a truly simple God has no attributes, since it is clear that attributes make something complex. Just as chapter 50 sets the stage for the following chapters by directing focus towards proper belief, chapter 51 presents the problem of attributes generally, outlining themes to which Maimonides returns later on. He divides attributes into two broad kinds, essential and accidental, and the accidental attributes are the main target of his critique. He says that it is immediately clear that an accident is not the same as the substance. A substance is something that exists in its own right, not as part of something else. An accident exists in something else, a substance, and depends on the substance for its existence: its existence is accidental as it does not exist in its own right. Anything with an accident is automatically complex, since it is divisible at the very least into substance and accident. A simple God therefore cannot have accidents.

A substance's essential attributes are simply explanations of the term that names the substance. These are either a name or parts of a definition. From one point of view, Maimonides considers them appropriate to God, as it is true to say that God is the Necessary Existent. He writes that an attribute can be 'the essence of the thing of which it is predicated, in which case it is an explanation of a term. We, in this respect, do not consider it impossible to predicate such an attribute of God, but do consider it impossible in another respect, as shall be made clear' (1:51, 113). Although it is true to say that God is a necessary existent, God is not thereby defined because the statement does not contain a genus and specific difference. When essential attributes define, they introduce multiplicity to an essence, so this is the respect in which they cannot be applied to God.

There is a puzzling statement in this chapter and accounting for it clarifies what Maimonides is up to. When he explains that it ought to be obvious that God has no attributes, and that the reason to prove otherwise is that people have mistakenly believed in such attributes, he likens the belief in attributes to other views that Aristotle took the trouble to prove even though they are clear, like the fact that motion exists. He writes, 'to this category belongs the denial of essential attributes to God, may He be exalted. For that denial is a primary intelligible, inasmuch as an attribute is not the essence of the thing of which it is predicated, but is a certain mode of the essence and hence an accident' (1:51, 112). This statement seems incoherent because it appears at first sight to say that essential attributes must be denied because essential attributes are accidental. Given that Maimonides distinguishes essential attributes from accidental ones, why does he say here that they are the same?

The point he is making is that the people he is here objecting to claim to believe that God has essential attributes, but those that they posit are actually accidents. He is not denying the distinction between different kinds of attributes but, instead, simply that God has such attributes: 'by denying the assertion that terms denoting accidents are attributes of the Creator, one does not deny the notion of accident' (1:51, 113). Since this chapter is partly aimed at setting the scene for what follows it, the statement is clarified when Maimonides returns to the issue several chapters later. He considers 'those who believe that there are essential attributes that may be predicated of the Creator – namely, that He is existent, living, possessing power, knowing, and willing' (1:56, 130). These terms all refer to attributes that are actually accidental rather than essential. The problem with those who posit essential attributes is therefore not only that they posit them in the first place. It is that they claim that God has essential attributes rather than accidental attributes, but they actually posit accidental attributes. Of course, they can say that these attributes are essential to God but, in order to be accurate, they would need to recognise the absolute difference between God and creatures, and Maimonides says that they do not. If a term like 'wise' or 'good' is understood to have a meaning that is in any way similar at all to that it has when used of humans, it has to be accidental. They could only be said to be essential if the words are used equivocally.

While chapter 51 follows from 50, it also demands further elaboration of the term 'attribute' and therefore leads into chapter 52, in which Maimonides classifies attributes into five kinds: definitions, parts of definitions, accidents, relations, actions. These are all positive attributes, attributes that can be predicated of something and ascribe a feature to that thing. Since the chapter is a part of the disquisition on divine attributes, it aims to explain which of these attributes can also be applied to God. The question addressed in this particular chapter concerns which of them, if any, can be said with a similar meaning when applied to both God and creatures. The first two are essential attributes, the other three non-essential. The essential attributes are, one, the definition and, two, parts of the definition. Since a definition indicates multiplicity, and God is not complex, God cannot be defined. As explained in Chapter 2, Aristotelian definitions contain two parts, genus and specific difference, and the definition refers to something's 'essence'. An object in the genus 'animal' that has 'rational' as its difference is a human being: the definition 'rational animal' explains what the nature of a human is. Each definition automatically introduces multiplicity because its purpose is to compare and contrast different kinds of things with each other. Furthermore, the essence depends on its parts. To understand the definition of a human, rational animal, you need first to understand what it is to be an animal. Since animal is the genus, it is in a sense prior to human because there can be animals that are not human. The human exists through being both rational and animal. If something is defined, it is explained through notions that are prior to it. However, Maimonides argues that God does not exist through anything else, being absolutely uncaused. Parts of definitions must also be denied of God. They can only be predicated of things that are composite, since they divide the defined thing into genus and species, which is a multiplicity and therefore opposed to God's unity. In sum, the first kind of attribute, definitions, are inappropriate to God, since God has no complexity. Maimonides even says that all 'who understand what they say' agree: 'this kind of attribute should be denied to God according to everybody' (1:52, 115). The same is true of the second kind of attribute, which is either genus or specific difference. These can only be attributed to creatures and it is absurd to predicate them of God, who is absolutely simple.

So much for essential attributes. Neither can God have accidental attributes. These are divided into those that indicate multiplicity, the third in his list, and those that do not. Since Maimonides has argued that God is absolutely simple, attributes implying multiplicity must be negated. In accord with chapter 51, he explains the different kinds of accidents that might be added to an object, such as colour, quantity, disposition, and habit, and denies that any can be predicated of God. All such attributes are attached to a substance, so anything that possesses them can be divided into substance and accident, which is a kind of composition. Therefore, accidents cannot be predicated of God.

The fourth kind of attribute is a relational attribute. Maimonides says that these present a different problem because 'this kind of attribute does not necessarily entail either multiplicity or change in the essence of the thing of which it is predicated' (1:52, 117). However, he then proceeds to say that with more thought, 'the fact that it is impossible becomes clear' (1:52, 117). A relation might not imply change because relations can change without any change in the thing being related to. For example, if you are on my left side, and I turn round, you would now be on my right even though you have not changed. Some relations are correlations. Examples of these are the relations between parent and child and master and slave. In order to be a parent someone must have a child, and vice-versa, so the related items depend on one another. Similarly, a slave is only a slave if in service to someone and a master can be a master only if ruling over a slave. These relations can also pertain without a change in one of the terms. It is possible to become a father even while being completely unaware of the change in status. Nevertheless, being a father depends on having a child. Maimonides explains that 'one of the properties of two correlated things is the possibility of inverting the statement concerning them while preserving their respective relations' (1:52, 117). He insists that God does not depend on anything in order to be a necessary existent and therefore cannot be one of the terms in a correlation. The point is similar to one I touched on in Chapter 4, when summarising Maimonides' claim that God's existence is not dependent on that of anything else: God does not exist by virtue of bringing other things into being.

Relations of these sorts pertain between created beings, since there needs to be some commonality between the two related things. There is no proportion between God and anything created whereby they can be compared or related. Maimonides explains that things can only be related if they are similar, so you can compare how bright a colour is with another instance of the same colour but not with an instance of a different one: 'one does not say that this red is more intense than this green or less or equally so' (1:52, 118). Even though they are both colours, there is no proportion between them because they are not the same species of colour. It would be even more difficult to try to compare a colour's brightness to the spiciness of a pepper. The more similar things are, the easier it is to tell them apart, which is why saying that two things are 'night and day' works well to emphasise the difference between them. It is easy to understand the phrase because night and day are similar things, both being periods of time. The more different things are, the more difficult it becomes to pin down exactly what the difference consists in, which is why the difference between night and five miles is not as easy to see. Five miles is more different from daytime than daytime is from night, being a length rather than a time. If God is so completely different from creatures that God cannot be defined, there is no way at all to compare and posit a relation between God and any creature that resembles the kinds of relations there are between one creature and another.

If God has no essential or accidental attributes, we cannot know God's nature. Nevertheless, Maimonides argues that we can know that God brings the world into being and is the only necessarily existing being. All of the sorts of relations in the fourth category must therefore be distinguished from the relationship that God does have to creatures, which is unique since God is the only creator. This creator–creature relationship cannot hold between any two created things. The relationship itself can be depicted only by predicating of God attributes of action, which are the fifth kind of predicates. We can say that things in the world are God's creatures, that God brings them into being and that they are therefore God's actions. Now, all the attributes that Maimonides treats in chapter 52 can be predicated of creatures. He asks which of them can also be predicated of God and argues that only attributes of action can. When Maimonides denies that God has attributes, he denies that attributes existing in the world are applicable to God. If they are to be predicated of God without the qualification that they are being used equivocally, he says, they must be interpreted as attributes of action. He says that God has no attributes other than attributes of action because by 'attribute', he means the sorts of features that creatures have. Anything other than an attribute of action needs to be qualified and said in a completely different way of God and creatures.

Chapter 53 continues by applying the claims made in 52 in order to criticise a particular approach, which is that of 'those who believe in the existence of attributes … The people in question have, as it were, divested God of corporeality but not of the modes of corporeality, namely, the accidents – I mean the aptitudes of the soul, all of which are qualities' (1:53, 120). Maimonides explains that these people aren't consistent because they recoil from saying that God has a body but assign to God attributes that depend on physicality. This chapter amounts to a critique of those who believe in divine attributes and, ultimately, believe that God possesses attributes related to matter, even if they don't realise that they are assuming God's corporeality. They then introduce multiplicity into the divine because they use adjectives to describe God, such as 'powerful', 'knowledgeable', 'alive', and 'willing', with a similar sense that these terms have when they are used of people. Since these represent distinct aspects in humans, and they stem from different potentialities and capabilities, it follows that those who are the subject of chapter 53's critique attribute various potentialities to God. Maimonides argues that these attributes cannot be assigned to God as if they are part of the divine essence, for that would introduce multiplicity. Instead, they should be used only 'in reference to the things that are created' (1:53, 122). If there are multiple attributes of action, it does not follow that there are multiple essential attributes. This is the mistake made by the opponents Maimonides takes on in chapter 53.

Maimonides explains that he is opposing those who were misled into believing that God has attributes by the literal, external sense of biblical passages, reminding us that the *Guide* is scriptural exegesis. There are many such passages, but the clearest might be that which is the subject of chapter 54, which deals with a pericope that appears to teach that God has thirteen separate attributes. Maimonides addresses the biblical figure of Moses, to whom the thirteen attributes are revealed in Exodus 34:6–7, and whom he calls here 'the master of those who know', someone who reached the highest possible level of human perfection. On Maimonides' telling, even he was unable to know God's essence. Maimonides explains that the divine attributes that he apprehended were attributes of action. The context is Moses' requests of God to 'show me your ways' and to 'show me your glory'. Maimonides takes the first question to be a request to know God's actions, to know what is created, and the second to be a request to know God's essence. He says that Moses is told that God's essence cannot be known but that God's actions can. Even though Moses' request was for knowledge of the divine essence, which he is denied, Maimonides says that he received a positive answer to both, inasmuch as there is no difference between God's glory and God's ways. Moses learned that God's essence is unknowable but that God's actions, the created world, can be known and that knowing these attributes of action is all the certain knowledge that can be ascertained about God.

At first glance, chapter 54 appears to be an exegetical interlude, but it is actually an important part of these chapters as it elaborates on 53, in which Maimonides states that 'every attribute that is found in the books of the deity, may He be exalted, is therefore an attribute of His action and not an attribute of His essence, or it is indicative of absolute perfection' (1:53, 121). Attributes of action are crucial both to say that God is the creator and also to characterise ideal human behaviour, and the chapter reflects the important connection between theology and the human goal. Through knowing God's actions, humans engage in proper worship of God, and knowing God's actions is equivalent to having knowledge of the world. Intellectual contemplation is the final human end and also the most authentic form of worship. It is not obvious how contemplating the intelligibles as products of God's activity, and therefore as divine attributes of action, leads us to characterise those actions. However, Maimonides says that they can be characterised as morals, although in that case the terms are used metaphorically.

> whenever one of His actions is apprehended, the attribute from which this action proceeds is predicated of Him, may He be exalted, and the name deriving from that action is applied to Him. For instance, one apprehends the kindness of His governance in the

production of the embryos of living beings, the bringing of various faculties to existence in them and in those who rear them after birth – faculties that preserve them from destruction and annihilation and protect them against harm and are useful to them in all the doings that are necessary to them. Now actions of this kind proceed from us only after we feel a certain affection and compassion, and this is the meaning of mercy.

Maimonides returns to the theme at the end of the Guide, when he explains that creation as a whole can be summed up through three attributes of action. God is said to act with loving kindness by bringing creatures into being, since loving kindness 'is excess in whatever matter excess is practiced. In most cases, however, it is applied to excess in beneficence' (3:53, 630). Creatures have no claim on God and can't be said to deserve existence. God has no duty to create so is going above and beyond by doing so. Similarly, God is said to be just, since justice involves giving someone exactly what is appropriate. Everything that is created is given what it needs in order to fulfil its goal, so God's creation is said to be just. Likewise, God is said to be 'judge' since judgement involves rewarding good or punishing wickedness, and Maimonides insisted, when explaining providence, that there is reward and punishment.

At the end of the *Guide*, Maimonides is revisiting the question of human perfection. There is no need to enter into detail here and recap the themes considered in Chapter 2, but it is worth recalling that human perfection involves acquiring all the virtues, moral and rational. In this context, human perfection involves a kind of imitation of God, since those who behave ethically do so by exercising exactly the kinds of characteristics that are figuratively attributed to divine actions. In his legal works, too, Maimonides includes 'imitating God's ways' as a separate commandment (*Character Traits*, 28). There is therefore an ethical dimension to Maimonides' claim that attributes of action can be predicated of God. Nevertheless, it is important not to lose sight of the fact that, in the chapters on which we are currently focusing, his primary concern when allowing attributes of action is logical: he is trying to avoid saying something false about God. Attributes of action can truly be predicated of God because God really is the creator. The relevant factors that enable us to use the word mercy are present, even though human mercy is not the same as divine mercy. When applying Maimonides' negative theology to these ideas as well, we need to remind ourselves that he is not saying that God is really a moral being, which would be another anthropomorphism. Unlike humans, who are moral beings because they possess virtuous habits and character traits, God does not act through a quality other than the divine essence, so to say that God acts with loving kindness is a metaphor. Maimonides writes that attributes of action do not refer to the 'habitus of an art that belongs to him who is described – as when you say a carpenter or a smith – inasmuch as this belongs to the species of quality, as we have mentioned' (1:52, 53).

In the following two chapters, 55 and 56, Maimonides continues to apply his insight that only actions can be attributed to God to mean something similar to what they mean when attributed to creatures, by further developing his critique of those who believe in divine attributes. He repeats the idea mentioned above, that a relation between two things requires a similarity of some sort. He then says that between God and creatures there is no relation and, therefore, no likeness. They are not completely different simply in the way that total opposites are. No difference, however great, reflects the absolute distinction between creator and creatures. To illustrate, he gives two examples of enormous differences and explains that such differences are between things of the same species. One is the difference in size between the entire universe and a mustard seed, and the other is the difference in heat between fire and wax melted in sunshine. In both cases, there is a common property, dimensions and temperature. No matter how great the difference, there is a similarity of some sort that enables the contrast to be made. Those Maimonides refutes in these two chapters depict divine attributes along these lines. 'According to what they think, the difference between these attributes and ours lies in the former being greater, more perfect, more permanent, or more durable than ours' (1:56, 130). However, if there is no relation between God and creatures, God cannot be differentiated from creatures in the way that they are distinguished from one another. If attributes like 'existent', 'living', 'knowing', 'powerful', and 'willing' are given the same meanings as they are when predicated of humans, they must be accidents.

These two chapters, 55 and 56, form a subunit. The first outlines some principles of natural science that are essential in the discussion of attributes that he undertakes in the second. Misunderstanding these physical principles leads to faulty theology, and the targets of Maimonides' critique in these two chapters appear to be kalām thinkers who reject Aristotelian physics. He says that while they claim that God's attributes are essential, 'all the attributes belonging to us are accidents according to the opinion of the Mutakallimūn. Would that I knew accordingly whence the likeness could come so that the divine and the human attributes could be comprised in the same definition and be used in a univocal sense, as these people believe' (1:56, 131). They go wrong because 'they think that the divine and human attributes are comprised in the same definition' (1:56, 131). If they are to be consistent, they would only agree to use these terms equivocally, so that the difference is not only that God is much better than we are. The distinction between creator and creature is simply of an entirely different order so that it is impossible even to compare God's power to human power or God's knowledge to human knowledge.

In chapter 57, Maimonides reaches the issue that lies behind his negative theology, divine simplicity and necessary existence. This is the idea to which I return in more detail below, in the second part of the current chapter, so a few words will suffice for the moment. As I outlined in Chapter 5, Maimonides argues that whatever is responsible for the world's existence must be a necessary existent and must be simple, containing no multiplicity whatsoever. The true meaning is not only that God is unique but that God is entirely indivisible. So far, in denying that God has attributes, Maimonides has been denying that God is made up of parts that can be classified. All definable beings are creatures in the world, beings that the system of categorising is designed to comprehend. And all accidents fall into the categories that distinguish things from one another. God does not fit into any of these schemes that we can use to understand things. Instead, we can say what God is not. Even when we say 'God is one', we are not saying that God is a single thing. Maimonides explains that it would be better to think of this statement in terms of negation too, since it is more accurate to say God is not among the kinds of things that can be counted. It is not simply that there is only one God, like there is only one planet Jupiter. God's absolute unity is therefore not reflected in any ordinary sense of the word 'one'. The same is true of the term 'eternal'. Maimonides explains that it would ordinarily refer to something temporal. An eternal being exists always and is therefore connected with time. God is not related to time, so saying that God is eternal should be interpreted negatively, to mean that God did not come into being. Such terms can only be used through 'a certain looseness of expression' (1:57, 133), by taking liberties with language.

To avoid saying something false about God, negations are of great value: 'they are those that must be used in order to conduct the mind toward that which must be believed with regard to Him, may He be exalted, for no notion of multiplicity can attach to Him in any respect on account of them; and, moreover, they conduct the mind toward the utmost reach that man may attain in the apprehension of Him' (1:58, 135). There is nevertheless a danger in focusing on negations. By simply negating a feature, it might seem that you are asserting the opposite. When applied to God, then, Maimonides explains that an attribute 'signifies the negation of the privation of the attribute in question' (1:58, 136). He has already explained that God cannot be deficient in any way. Instead, 'all His perfections must exist in actuality, and nothing may belong to Him that exists potentially in any respect whatever' (1:55, 128). But Maimonides cannot mean simply that all God's potentialities are actualised and he continues by saying that 'one must likewise of necessity deny, with reference to Him, His being similar to any existing thing' (1:55, 128). Saying that God lacks potentiality because everything in God is actual could imply that there are such potentialities in the first place, even if they are said to be eternally actualised. In Maimonides' view, this is wrong. God has no potential features but also no actualised potentialities. Negating privations of perfections in God must therefore be distinguished from asserting the perfections themselves. This strategy is what Maimonides uses to show that God cannot be subsumed under any category of perfection. Saying that God has no privations is only appropriate if it is accompanied by negating the perfections too, because the only kinds of perfections we could intelligibly assert would be those that are similar to created perfections. Neither potentialities nor actualities, privations nor perfections, are really applicable to a necessary being. We can say that certain things must be true of a necessary being, that there is no distinction between essence and existence nor any complexity at all to the divine being, and we can explain that we have no perceptual apparatus to understand such a being. When using terms like 'one' and 'eternal' of God, these terms must be qualified so that their inadequacy is clear.

Scholars usually focus on Maimonides' enthusiasm for negative attributes rather than what underpins them, and there is good reason for doing so. Negative theology has important ramifications for religious faith. As Kenneth Seeskin has emphasised in a number of places, it is a corrective to idolatrous tendencies arising from natural human desires and from the society around us.[2] If only God is worthy of worship, and negative theology teaches us that God is completely unlike anything in the created world, monotheistic faith demands that we constantly guard against any hint of worshipping something worldly. Negative theology challenges us to make sure that we do not assign ultimate value to anything, whether it be power, beauty, wealth or possessions, a political entity, a charismatic individual, or an ideology. Anything that can be captured or approximated in either thought or intelligible language cannot be God and making it an object of absolute commitment is tantamount to idolatry. Since Maimonides argues that proper worship involves studying God's actions, the natural world, and understanding the connections between creatures, his brand of monotheism also involves guarding against assigning greater importance to anything than it actually has. Increasing a creature's value or assigning it some sort of independent spiritual worth draws attention away from God as the sole creator and the only proper worshipful target.

Despite negative theology's importance, it is possible to go too far. The conclusion reached in the arguments presented in Chapter 5 was that God is a necessary existent, and that certainly seems like an assertion. On Maimonides' account, divine simplicity is secured to the utmost degree through this distinction between the Necessary Existent and created, contingent existents. But he is not denying God's unlimited perfection. His arguments show that God is not restricted in the way that creaturely perfections are. In his view, they are not captured by the words we use because what we mean by words like 'good' is always conditioned by whatever is said to be good. We do not use the term 'goodness itself' to talk about a good creature. Unlike God, no creature can be entirely perfect, since every creature's perfection is limited to the kind of thing it is. Maimonides claims that the only path open to us is therefore to negate privations of perfections.

Elaborating divine simplicity a little further shows that Maimonides' position is in some ways less negative than it appears. His argument is not that words are inappropriate because there is no God, or that the being of 'God' is completely empty. Rather, they cannot reflect God adequately because they introduce limitations, and God is unlimited. True, God is not a thing because God creates everything. Nevertheless, denying that the word 'exists' can apply to God in any normal sense is not the same as asserting that God is not. In Maimonides' view, words cannot reflect God because we can only understand the ways in which they relate to our experience, and that experience is restricted to created beings. Even terms that indicate perfections are inapplicable because 'everything you affirm is a perfection only with reference to us' (1:59, 139). Ultimately, this is at the root of a critique of Maimonides' theology made by many who deem it too negative. For example, Aquinas argues that the real meaning of some terms should be distinguished from what can be understood by them. We saw an example in the way that we use the word 'good'. The meaning we understand is limited to a particular kind of goodness that is delineated by the sort of thing that is said to be good. However, in no case is 'goodness' itself predicated of any of the things we understand. The same is true of other terms that are considered transcendentals, which means that they are not limited to any particular kind of thing or category but transcend and therefore range across them. Beauty is one such example, as it means something different when said of a piece of music than when said of a person's character or a mathematical proof. None of these things contains beauty itself even if they are all beautiful in their own ways. Maimonides does not explicitly make the distinction that Aquinas uses. He might not have thought of it, even though there is no reason to think that he would have objected to it, but his reticence can also be explained by the polemical nature of these chapters dealing with divine attributes, in which the purpose is to defend divine simplicity. So, while a number of medieval thinkers disagreed with Maimonides, the criticism made by philosophers such as Thomas Aquinas and Gersonides concerned whether some words can be appropriately used to refer to God, not whether or not God can be understood. Ultimately, these critics argue that such words, indicating perfections, are properly used of God but they cannot be understood by natural human reason.

The criticism highlights a problem that Maimonides faces, which is that a negative theologian is faced with a peculiar situation. Usually, coming to know something involves learning about all the attributes that thing could possibly possess. If you understand what the essence of something is, you don't only know that it has these essential features, as if they could exist apart from its accidental features. If all you knew was the essence, you would not really know the thing very well. When you know what something is, you know all the different features it can have. Therefore, the more attributes you understand can be attached to something, the better you are said to know that thing. Once you understand that a human is a rational animal, you know more than only the definition because you cannot understand 'rational animal' as if it can be abstracted from everything that rational animals do. Proper understanding involves knowing all that is implied by animality and rationality, including the activities of all the different parts of the soul, vegetative, motive, and rational. It involves knowing that a person has a capacity to run, play, laugh, create, debate, and all the other activities in which people engage. Knowing more attributes that an object can have therefore leads to a fuller understanding of what that thing is. The essence allows for the features that an object of a particular species has or can have. A cat can have a particular colour, can hunt or play with a ball of string, but it cannot be entirely transparent. A window can be transparent but cannot hunt. In each case, the features are indicated by the subject's nature and as you understand more of the features that can be predicated of the subject, the better you can be said to know it. Maimonides writes, 'the thing of which attributes are predicated becomes more particu-larised with every increase in attributes that are predicated of it, and he who predicates these attributes accordingly comes nearer to the apprehension of the true reality of the thing in question' (1:59, 138).

Negative theology appears to teach that the opposite is true when it comes to knowing God: 'you come nearer to the apprehension of Him, may He be exalted, with every increase in the negations regarding Him; and you come nearer to that apprehension than he who does not negate with regard to Him that which, according to what has been demonstrated to you, must be negated' (1:59, 138). However, in order to understand that the negations are necessary, there has to be some way of articulating the controlling notion that underpins them. You need to understand why attributes have to be negated because you need to understand that the controlling notion rules them out. This controlling notion is Maimonides' claim that God is necessary and, therefore, entirely simple.

2. Negative Theology: Existence and the Fullness of Being

Maimonides is clear that there is an absolute difference between God's being and that of creatures. He argues that God is the only necessarily existing being and God's necessity is expressed in there being no difference between God's essence and God's existence. However, in order to see how this distinguishes God from the world, we need first of all to think about how to charac-terise existence generally. What sort of property is it, if it is even a property at all? Unfortunately for us, Maimonides does not say much about it. As is his general strategy throughout the *Guide*, which we have encountered in earlier chapters, he does not go into detail in order to explain these issues. Instead, he leaves readers to figure a lot out for themselves. In order to test and train, and also to make sure that the *Guide's* truths are reserved for those who are capable and deserving, readers are expected to think and research independently. Whether or not Maimonides intentionally explains this particular issue tersely for precisely the purpose of hiding or testing is uncertain. While he would have hoped readers would be familiar with discussions like that in Avicenna's *Metaphysics*, it is also possible that he didn't see the need to explain in detail because he considered it unnecessary to elaborate, or that he simply hadn't questioned certain presuppositions he made about the nature of existence. What he does say is this:

> It is known that existence is an accident attaching to what exists. For this reason, it is something that is superadded to the quiddity of what exists. This is clear and necessary with regard to everything the existence of which has a cause. Hence its existence is something that is superadded to its quiddity. (1:57, 132)

Even though he is here characterising the existence that pertains to creatures, the chapter's context is his attempt to distinguish creatures from God. The next sentences explain that even the most basic distinction found in all that is not divine is to be denied of God, which is that between essence and existence, a distinction that was crucial in the arguments of Chapter 5.

> As for that which has no cause for its existence, there is only God, may He be magnified and glorified, who is like that. For this is the meaning of our saying about Him, may He be exalted, that His existence is necessary. Accordingly, His existence is identical with His essence and His true reality, and His essence is His existence. (1:57, 132)

Given the philosophical accounts of existence that hold sway in recent times, Maimonides' own assumptions need to be questioned. Indeed, if they are to be considered philosophically intelligible at all, they will have to be defended. Otherwise, many philosophers today simply dismiss the claim that there can be a necessarily existing being, with one distinguished scholar of Aquinas going as far as saying that it is 'sophistry and illusion'.[3] Maimonides' statements accord with some of the things that Avicenna wrote about the topic, and Aquinas also followed them. Even if Aquinas' approach is not identical to Maimonides', as the abovementioned objection to his negative theology indicates, there is some similarity between their approaches.

Let's begin by considering what Maimonides means when he says that existence is an accident. At this point, readers are faced with a number of difficulties. Aside from the methodological difficulty generated by the fact that Maimonides does not explain it any further, the philosophical issues that his statements raise need to be addressed: it is not clear how existence can be an accident and, furthermore, it seems to render the very idea of a being that is identical with its existence incoherent. I'll return to the second of these two problems below. It will only be clear why it arises once the first has been addressed, so I begin now by explaining what the difficulty with characterising existence as an accident is and how that difficulty can be met. Again, I repeat that Maimonides himself does not address the question directly.

The first difficulty arises from the very claim that existence is an accident. At first blush, this seems absurd. Recall that an accident is something that exists in an object and depends on the object's existence for its own: accidents inhere in substances. If the accident depends on the substance, saying that existence is an accident seems to lead to circularity. Were existence an accident, existence would require a pre-existing subject, but that is impossible. If the subject is to receive existence as an accident, it must be assumed already to have existence but it is that very existence that is supposed to be added on afterwards. The problem is nicely illustrated by one of the different ways in which Aristotle explains what it means to be an accident. He says that it is something that 'can possibly belong and not belong to one and the same thing, whatever it may be. For instance, it is possible for "being seated" to belong and not belong to the same thing.'[4] Clearly, a person can sit at one time and stand at another without ceasing to be a person and, if existence is an accident of this sort, it can belong to something or not belong to it. If existence is accidental, shouldn't an existing person then be able to pop in and out of existence, similar to the way in which that person can sit or stand? Not necessarily.

Aristotle explains the term 'accident' in different ways. In the same place he also explains that it is something that 'is not a definition, a unique property, or a genus, but yet belongs to the subject'. This account turns out to be more promising for our purposes. Nevertheless, the first way of defining accident, as that which 'can possibly belong and not belong to one and the same thing', has an advantage, Aristotle says. It is easy to understand because you don't need to know the meanings of 'definition', 'unique property', or 'genus' in order to do so. However, it is also potentially misleading. There are accidents that are inseparable, like the colour black belonging to a raven, which is an accident even if all ravens must always be black.

The simpler of Aristotle's two explanations has another advantage for our purposes, which is that it helps clarify how odd it seems to be to say that existence is an accident and that, if the statement makes sense, the notion of accident must be understood differently in the case of existence from the way it is understood of all other accidents. The problem is that if an accident depends on something, that thing must be prior to its accident. But if existence has to be assumed, it cannot be added as an accident because, if it is an added accident, it should not be assumed. Take a red fence, for example. The fence can exist before it is painted red and it could change colour were someone to paint it again. The accident red is posterior to the fence itself, and can belong or not belong to the fence. However, the important point isn't simply that the fence can change its colour. What is important about the priority of substance to accident is its logical priority rather than its chronological priority. If someone has blue eyes, the colour might never change. Nevertheless, it's easy to see that the colour is logically posterior to the eyes, inasmuch as the colour depends on the eye rather than the other way around. There are eyes that are not blue but there is no instance of the colour blue that is not instantiated in a substance. It is not necessary that a substance be one particular colour rather than another, but it is necessary that every colour inheres in some substance. If a colour doesn't exist as a colour of something, it doesn't exist at all.

In light of this background, if existence is to be considered an accident, it must be an accident of a highly unusual sort and the challenge will be to explain what it means to characterise existence as accidental. As it happens, Maimonides presents his own description of accident. When explaining that God has no accidental attributes, he writes as follows: 'for every notion super-added to an essence is an adjunct to it and does not perfect its essence, and this is the meaning of accident' (1:51, 113). Inseparable accidents are also covered by this account, as is anything else that is not part of the essence.

While Maimonides' statement does not explain how existence can be an accident, it enables us to meet the obvious criticism that was levelled against him, that what he says is added only after-wards is tacitly assumed to be prior. In doing so, Maimonides' description points the way we need to go in order to think further about the question. It indicates that the reason existence is accidental is not that it can either belong or not belong. Instead, in order to fulfil his criterion, existence has to be something that does not perfect a substance's essence. The accidental feature cannot be part of the substance's definition. If it is a property that can really be distinguished from essence, it fulfils Maimonides' criterion for being considered an accident. Firstly, then, we can recall that Maimonides does indeed consider a thing's existence to be really distinct from its essence, which is the reason he argues that nothing can account for its own existence. One of the arguments for God's existence outlined in Chapter 5 depends on the claim that essence and existence are distinct. To repeat the point, the distinction is reflected in the fact that an answer to the question what something is differs from the answer to the question whether something is. Existence is not taken as part of the definition and is therefore distinguished from essence.

Now, if it is really possible to distinguish essence from existence, questions about existence arise. Is it a real property and, if so, what sort of property is it? Many philosophers today, and some in Maimonides' time too, claim that existence cannot be a real property even though it is not strictly a part of something's essence. In their views, existence cannot be a real accident even though, because it does not perfect the essence, it seems to satisfy Maimonides' requirements. To be more precise, existence is said not to be a property of individuals since no property can be ascribed to an individual unless it already exists. Individuals cannot either have or lack existence since, were they to do so, it would be possible to attribute nonexistence to a particular thing. But if it does not exist it is not an individual in the first place. Nonexistence can be said of kinds, however, like dragons or dinosaurs. Existence is therefore held by many philosophers to be a general property rather than a real property of individuals. In response, it might be pointed out that existence can be a real property even if nonexistence is not. It will be an unusual property, however, since it cannot either attach or not attach to something and therefore calls for an account of attachment different from other properties, which I will come to below.

Another apparent difficulty arises because a property of an individual characterises a feature that belongs to that individual, something that can be used to describe it by adding to the information we have about what the individual is and what it is like. Existence does not add any such feature, it is claimed. Existence is not an empirical feature of an existing object, so the slogan 'existence is not a predicate' is often used to indicate that existence does not add anything and, therefore, existence cannot be a real property. An accident is a property, and is predicated of a substance; if the modern slogan is accepted, Maimonides should not be entitled to say that existence is an accident, a property of individuals. For thinkers such as Maimonides, existence is indeed a real property of things, even though it does not attach to things in the same way as other properties, by depending on objects for its actuality. Regarding this point, it seems that Maimonides disagrees with the common idea holding that 'exists is not a predicate' and 'existence is not a property'. I will return to this second difficulty below. It will turn out that Maimonides could also have rejected this aspect of the objection, and that a solution to the first question opens the way to showing that he could also have rejected the second.

Regarding the first difficulty, the problem arises because, if Maimonides' statements about existence are to make sense, it must be possible for existence to be a property attached to an individual without being posterior to it. To see how that might be possible, we need to be yet clearer about what exactly the problem is. It is not enough simply to say that a substance is prior to its accidents, since there are two different ways in which it is prior. In order to be instantiated, accidents depend on the substances in which they inhere – accidents depend on substances for their existence – and this is the respect in which the question above was raised and the difficulty explained; they also depend on the substance to be individuated, in order to be distinguished from other instances of the same sort of accident. This second feature needs to be explained further.

In order to clarify, let me return to the image of a painted fence. We saw that the fence is prior to its colour inasmuch as the fence's redness depends on the fence in order to exist. The fence is therefore prior in respect of existence and actuality. Additionally, the redness depends on the fence in order to be distinct from other instances of the same colour. If a fence and an adjacent chair are both painted red from the same can, the redness in the fence is distinguished from that of the chair because it is painted onto a different object; each would have its own instance of redness distinct from that of any other instance. The fence is therefore prior to its colour also in respect of individuation. These two features hold for accidents generally. They are posterior to their substances in these two respects, in respect of actuality and in respect of individuation.

The charge levelled above against Maimonides' statement that existence is an accident, that it makes existence dependent on a substance that must already exist, relates only to the first of the two. It is based on the intuition that an accident depends on its subject's existence. Because of this dependence, Aristotle was able to say that an accident can either belong or not belong to a subject, like when a person is standing or sitting. Existence cannot be like an accident in this regard because an accident of such a sort assumes the existence of its subject. However, in the second respect, existence can indeed be likened to an accidental feature. The existence of an individual is distinct from that of any other individual by belonging to the instantiated particular. A distinction between the existence of one individual and that of another relies on the individuals in question, in a similar way to that in which the distinction between the different instances of redness relies on the individual fences. My existence can only be different from that of John's if we both already exist, for if there is no me, there is nothing to be distinct.

This criticism is considered sufficient to rule out the possibility that existence is an accident. However, it need not be. Again, if existence is accidental, it must be a very peculiar kind of accident. It must be unique inasmuch as it is not posterior to a substance both in respect of actuality and of individuality. Instead, it could be posterior only in respect of individuality while being prior in respect of actuality. If so, it would still satisfy the alternative description of accident, mentioned by both Aristotle and Maimonides, that an accident is something that is distinct from the essence of its subject. Maimonides' characterisation of existence as an accident is therefore useful but easily misunderstood. In order to defend it, there is a need to find a way of portraying this connection between essence and existence that preserves the relationship outlined here. Existence must be logically prior to a subject in terms of actuality but posterior in terms of individuality. For example, a person's existence is distinct from that of other people by virtue of belonging to this individual, so her existence depends on the person for her individuation. But in order to exist in the first place, the person depends on her existence. If it is possible to think of existence as relating to existing things in a way that preserves its posteriority in respect of actuality, while at the same time admitting that the existence of individual features depends on their substances in order to be differentiated from other instances of the same features in different objects, the challenge can be met. If existence can be depicted in such a way, the objection that existence cannot be an accident because it must be prior to its subject is not decisive.

It is clear that Maimonides considers existence to be separate from essence, and that essences are represented by definitions. An essence is a kind of limit, which is picked out by a definition. A definition delineates an essence by delimiting its subject to a particular genus and a particular species, thereby restricting the essence. The relationship between existence and essence is therefore not one of inhering: unlike other non-essential properties, existence does not inhere in its subject. Instead, it must be depicted in a different way. A recent philosopher, Barry Miller, conceived an alternative analogy to 'inherence' to illustrate the relationship.[5] He argues that the relationship between an existing thing and its essence can be likened to that between a substance and its bound, which, together, result in an instance of existence. The bound restricts the existence possessed by an individual by limiting the kinds of properties it can have. Only properties admitted by the essence can be predicated of it. For example, a cat can be furry or friendly but cannot fly or photosynthesize. The properties that can be affirmed of the cat are delimited by its bound, which is signified by its definition. Other objects have other properties, which are similarly limited by their respective bounds.

An image that can help illustrate this idea is that of a block of ice from which individual chunks can be separated. After being chopped off the whole, an individual piece of ice is a piece that exists within the surface that binds it. The bound individuates the ice and sets it apart from other chunks of the same sort. The ice therefore depends on its bound for its individuality. However, the individual is posterior to the entire block and depends on the block's prior existence for its own. Thinking of the individual as that which is within its bound can therefore illustrate how something can be prior to a property in terms of individuation while remaining posterior in terms of actuality. It is therefore an appropriate image by which to represent the relationship between an individual and its existence.

Since this idea of a bound is an analogy, it is not a perfect representation of the relationship between essence and existence. Whereas the chunk of ice is cut away from a larger block that exists independently, the same is obviously not true of a person's existence. There is no prior block of existence from which the person's existence is detached. Instead, the relevant priority that an object's existence has over its bound is purely logical, not chronological or ontological. What is important is that, since existence can be conceived in a similar way, the analogy of an object and its bound illustrates how it is possible for something to be logically posterior to its existence. There is therefore no need to say that, because an object must presume its existence in order to possess any features, existence cannot be a real non-essential feature.

Once the relationship between essence and existence is depicted as equivalent to that between a bound and what is bounded, there is no need to accept the common objection that, because existence doesn't add anything to a substance, it cannot be a real property. A person might have different properties, such as wisdom, musicality, being six feet tall, or having yellow hair, and all of these tell you something about what the person is like. Existence doesn't: it is simply the precondition for her being like anything at all. This is the problem mentioned above, and summed up by the slogan 'existence is not a property'. However, the problem assumes that if existence is a property, it must be a property like others, added to a prior substance. Given the idea that existence is a bounded property, it need not be posterior and does not need to add something to a pre-existing substance in order to be a real property. In that case, Maimonides is justified in characterising it as an accident, by which he means that it is a non-essential property, and the objection does not hold.

Maimonides' statement that existence is an accident can therefore be seen to make sense. However, as I mentioned above, his purpose is to distinguish creaturely existence from that of God by arguing that in God there is no distinction between essence and existence and that God's existence is therefore necessary. Just as his comment about existence is very short and required some investigation, so too is what he says about God's existence because explaining existence in creatures does not seem to help. On the contrary, it seems to render absurd the notion that any existence can be necessary. How, then, does an analysis of the existence possessed by creatures help clarify the absolute difference between God's existence and creaturely existence and is it possible to defend the claim that there is a necessary existent from the objection that it is incoherent? It can only be defended if sense can be made of the idea that, unlike existing beings, God's essence and existence are not related as a bound to that which is bounded, there being no difference between them. In the quotation cited at the beginning of this section of the present chapter, Maimonides writes that God's 'existence is identical with His essence and His true reality, and His essence is His existence'. In light of his own claim that existence is an accidental feature, this sentence does not seem to make sense. For there to be an existing being, something must restrict the existence and individuate it: its existence is not the restriction but that which is restricted by the essence. The existence itself cannot be the bound because it would then be bounding itself, and that which is not in itself restricted would be a restriction. Does this problem render the notion of a necessary being absurd? For Maimonides, it does not. These observations would not count as evidence against a necessary being but would instead reflect the absolute distinction between God and creatures.

There are two further ideas that need to be taken into account to make sense of the claim that God's essence and existence are identical. One is that there is a hierarchy of being and the other is that the limit of a scale can differ absolutely from the scale's members.

The idea that there is a hierarchy of existence is unpopular today, since it is opposed to the view that existence adds nothing and therefore cannot be a real property. If existence is not a real property, there is no difference between the various existences of disparate kinds of things. Of course, there is a difference between the instance of existence of an amoeba and that of a human, since they are different things. However, on this view, there is no conceptual difference between the existence of one and the existence of another. Existence is everywhere the same. While this is the prevailing view in modern times, it was not always so dominant, and it is unnecessary in light of the above account of the relationship between essence and existence. Many medieval thinkers held that there were modulations in being, and often even thought that there can be a hierarchy of being. Maimonides' statements about existence indicate that he accepted that there are degrees of being, an idea that was in his time commonplace.

Is it possible to make sense of such a hierarchy? Consider hierarchies of particular kinds. In Chapter 3, I explained that something is considered good inasmuch as it exists with all the properties that it is supposed to have, inasmuch as its form is actualised. So, for example, an apple with all the features of a fully grown apple would be a better apple than one that is not yet ripe or has rotted. It exists qua apple in a better way. There is a sense in which there can be a hierarchy of apples, one being more or less edible than another, and other things can also be rated according to how well they embody the form they represent. The reason you are able to judge whether one thing is better than another is that you know what the thing is. The more complex the kinds of things you are trying to arrange, the more difficult it becomes to agree on the order of things within the hierarchy. In some cases, there might even be a degree of subjectivity. Listeners might disagree over which recording of a particular piece of music is better. Most will agree, however, that professional musicians play the piece better than an amateur who has only just begun to learn it. The musical recordings might also have objective features that make them easily distinguishable, fewer mistakes or greater pathos for instance. A musician who knows the piece will be better able to tell how well it is being played than someone who has never heard it before and knows little about music. There might also be a difficulty deciding which of two people are more virtuous, especially since a variety of different character traits would have to be taken into account. Nevertheless, the idea that there can in principle be better and worse people or musicians is not opposed by the fact that it is often difficult, and sometimes perhaps impossible, to decide which is superior. In sum, since creatures have a bound, an essence that is captured by a definition, they can be characterised in various ways, and because they can be described in particular ways, they can also be compared in those ways and rated according to how well or badly they live up to a certain feature.

An obvious problem arises if you try to apply this idea to existence in general. Arranging fruits generally according to their degree of crunchiness seems different from arranging them according to their level of existence. An excellent apple is a better apple than an excellent orange, but it does not seem to have a greater amount of existence. To have a scale of ordered things, you need a characteristic of some sort to define the scale, and you would have to be able to say what that characteristic is. However, since existence has been distinguished from essence, and a substance is characterised by its essence, existence itself seems not to fit on a scale. Existence isn't a characteristic that distinguishes one being from another. Things are rated as better or worse instances of something in particular. And what they are depends on their bound, the essence, not on what is bounded, the existence.

Despite these objections, those who argue that existence is a real property can assert that different sorts of beings can be rated according to their existence per se rather than simply according to their existence as a particular kind of thing. And depicting an individual as a bound of its existence facilitates this move. Thinking of existence as bounded allows us to depict differences in the existence possessed by different beings. Some individuals have more properties than others and can therefore be said to have a richer form of being in the world. If there are such differences, it is also possible to ask whether individuals can be graded according to the amount of existence they have. It then becomes possible to think of individuals as restricting their existence to a greater or a lesser degree, so that the existence had by one individual can differ from that of another. Of course, the two instances differ since they are different individuals, but, in addition, they are not equally rich instances of existence. The kind of existence had by an inanimate piece of wood differs from the kind of existence had by a human and the difference is in how they are actualised by their respective bounds. A hierarchy of being is therefore intelligible, as a hierarchy of diminishing restrictiveness. Note that arranging creatures on some sort of scale of being is not necessarily to say that one kind of creature is more important or more valuable than another. If apples and amoebae are at different levels on the scale, it does not follow that one is more important than the other, nor does humans having a less restrictive bound than hens, since humans are rational, automatically make humans morally better, even if they have a greater share in existence. It is still possible to be a very bad human and a very good hen. The point is simply that one can be said to have a less restrictive bound, allowing for a richer kind of life and that, if existing beings can be said to have a greater or lesser share of existence, it is in principle possible to arrange them according to their share.

If beings can be arranged according to how restrictive their kinds of essences are, it makes sense to ask what might be at the top of the scale. Is there something that can possess existence to the greatest possible degree and what would such a thing be like? Most importantly for present purposes, would that being be necessary and, therefore, would it be identical with God? In Maimonides' view, the answer has to be no. Recall that the difference Maimonides draws between them is that God lacks the distinction between essence and existence. God therefore lacks the feature characteristic of things on the scale. God cannot simply have the widest possible boundary, allowing for the greatest share of existence. Everything on a particular scale must possess the features characteristic of that scale. Therefore, everything that is on the scale of existent things must possess existence. It is characteristic of everything on the scale that it be bounded. That which possesses the least restrictive possible bound will have the greatest share of existence, will be the most fully existent being. It will nonetheless still be an existing being with a distinct essence restricting its existence. By contrast, God has no boundary at all. God's existence cannot be restricted by anything other than itself, which is to say that it is not restricted at all. If there is no distinction between essence and existence in God, God's existence is entirely unbound.

However, this claim does not seem to make sense. If an individual is characterised as a bound, expressed by the definition, and that which is bounded, there can be no individual in which no distinction between the two can be made. It would therefore seem that there cannot be an entirely unrestricted being, since whatever is at the top of a scale can only possess the features of that scale to the utmost degree. And everything that belongs to that scale is limited to the features of that scale. Something that is at the top of a hierarchy of one kind of fruit, for example, which is the most perfect possible example of its kind, would not possess all the good features of another, simply because they are different things. A perfect apple cannot possess the features of a perfect orange, nor of a perfectly formed hyena. All creatures have a nature that limits what they have the potential to be. Anything at the top of such a scale therefore cannot be unlimited. The being that could, in theory, embody the most superior kind of existence could not be necessary because in order for it to be an existing thing at all, however perfect, it must be delimited somehow. Nothing in a hierarchy can be completely unrestricted. It must be restricted to those properties that define the scale. No individual's existence can be unrestricted since to be an individual is precisely to be restricted to a particular instance of existence. Therefore, any individual at the top of the scale of existence would still have to be delimited, even if it is the most perfect possible instance of existence, possessing existence in the maximal possible degree. It would be at the top of a scale that is characterised by the definition that delimits the kinds of things belonging to that scale. If God's perfections are depicted in this way, they would be subject to Maimonides' criticisms of those who believe in attributes.

In sum, the very idea of a necessary being having no definable bound, indistinguishable from its existence, seems to be incoherent. No individual can be unrestricted because that would mean that it has no nature at all. On the one hand, Maimonides would be able to grant as much, simply by denying that God is an individual with a nature other than the divine existence. On the other hand, asserting that God's existence differs from that of creatures by virtue of not possessing the feature that characterises existent beings might leave you wondering whether there is any way to make sense of unrestricted being.

A necessary existent that possesses no restricting essence other than its existence can be thought of in line with another analogy designed to show that a scale's limit can differ absolutely from the scale's members. It is possible to distinguish two different ways in which a scale can end. The first is at a limit that possesses the scale's features to a maximal or minimal degree. In these cases, the limit is the same sort of thing as other members of the scale, only more perfect. The speed of light is an example. It is the quickest possible speed and therefore a speed limit. However, a limit can also differ from the kinds of things that it limits. The lower limit of speed, for example, is not a speed at all, but is instead complete rest. Even though it is not itself a speed, motionlessness is that in which decreasing speeds end. Another example is a polygon. There seems to be no upper limit to how many sides can be added to a polygon. Should such a limit be reached, and another side be added, the polygon would turn into a circle, so would no longer be part of the scale it has now transcended. In these cases, the defining feature of the scale's members no longer exists. An object at rest has no speed and a circle has no sides. It is as if the features that make the members of the scale what they are have been multiplied out of existence. The resulting limit is a different kind of thing from the members of the scale it limits so it is no longer a maximum or minimum of that particular scale.

The limit of a scale of existence should be thought of in this way. If there is something that possesses being to the fullest possible degree, it would have to be unlimited to a particular kind of existence; restricting it would automatically mean that it does not possess the fullness of existence. As the limit is the defining feature of the suggested scale of being, the characteristic of the scale would no longer apply. Since the characteristic of a creature is that its existence is limited by essence, a being without the feature that represents creatures has no difference between essence and existence, and such a being is also unrestricted. This is exactly how Maimonides characterises the difference between contingent beings and a necessary existent. He is not saying that there is an object that is identical with its existence, since God is not an object at all. Rather, should there be a truly necessarily existent being – and Maimonides thinks that there must be in order to account for the fact that anything at all exists – it must be absolutely unrestricted and unlimited. It must therefore be entirely different from any created being, since to be created is already to be restricted in some way. Anything that is limited in such a way cannot possess the fullness of being but, instead, a particular kind of being. God's existence is not limited to any particular kind since it has no essence other than the existence itself. A necessary being, characterised as lacking a distinction between essence and existence, is completely unrestricted and, since the existence is not attached, it is necessary. Maimonides' distinguishing God from everything on the basis that God lacks the limitations inherent to all individuals is therefore an intelligible way of saying that God's existence is necessary and that God is the uniquely simple, unrestricted being, undefinable and not subject to any sort of characterisation or qualification, absolutely different to anything that can be conceived or imagined.

It is important to keep in mind that Maimonides is not saying that what is an accident in creatures is essential to God. The difference cannot be simply that creatures have existence while God *is* existence. Instead, God's existence must be of a completely different sort, so much so that the term 'existence' means something entirely different when used of God. If we are tempted to say that 'God exists', Maimonides reminds us that attributes must be denied of God, so 'existence' is said equivocally of contingent beings, on the one hand, and the necessary being, on the other: 'the term "existent" is predicated of Him, may He be exalted, and of everything that is other than He, in a purely equivocal sense' (1:56, 131). A necessary existent of this kind is sometimes referred to as 'subsistent existence'. To say that something subsists is to say that it exists independently, that it is a substance. Since the substances with which we are familiar do not exist simply inasmuch as they are what they are, they do not exist in their own right. Instead, they exist contingently, which is to say that they are caused to exist by something else.

Distinguishing necessary from contingent existents grounds Maimonides' negative theology. Because of the absolute difference, 'everything that can be ascribed to God, may He be exalted, differs in every respect from our attributes, so that no definition can comprehend the one thing and the other' (1:35, 80). Language does not adequately reflect God, since understanding the words we use relies on having some way of conceiving that to which they apply. 'Know that when you make an affirmation ascribing another thing to Him, you become more remote from Him in two respects: one of them is that everything you affirm is a perfection only with reference to us, and the other is that He does not possess a thing other than His essence, which, as we have made clear, is identical with His perfections' (1:59, 139). There cannot be any distinction between God's perfections because there is no distinct essence by which to differentiate them. A necessary existent must possess the fullness of being, with all its perfections uncreated and unlimited, and Maimonides claims that such perfections cannot be captured at all by the language we use about things that we understand. The best we can hope for is to understand as much as is possible for humans and also to recognise and understand the intellect's limitations.

7

Diverse Interpretations and Disputed Instructions

Reading the Guide for the Perplexed

Today, Maimonides remains one of the most referenced Jewish religious authorities ever. His influence on, among others, Thomas Aquinas, Meister Eckhart, Leibniz and Spinoza assures his renown in the West and he is widely recognised in the Muslim world, even though he seems not to have had much impact on the Islamic tradition. In Jewish circles, his *Code* is a touchstone in halakhic discussions, and his philosophical works are also used as an example for those with very different ideological commitments. Traditionalist readers often point to his thirteen principles as the quintessential expression of Jewish faith, even though they were debated for centuries, as they were written to delineate what a follower of rabbinic Judaism ought to believe, while others focus on the many statements or ideas that accord with contemporary sensibilities.[1] Undoubtedly, such diverse readings find their support in Maimonides' rich and complex body of writing, but they are also partly motivated by his dominant standing in the Jewish world. In this chapter, I will touch on some of the major ways in which Maimonides' influence was felt and I will then explain something about what makes the *Guide* in particular such a fertile work for extremely varied interpretations. The second of these tasks is presented partly to justify approaching Maimonides as a philosopher in the way that I have. Throughout this introduction, I have offered an interpretation of Maimonides' thought that preserves his explicit doctrines. I have taken him at his word when he claims to hold a certain position, although I have indicated that there are occasions when such a reading is contested. Among Maimonides' interpreters, it is extremely common to claim that he hid his real opinion. In the second part of this chapter, I will explain some of the textual support that people use to argue for the view that he is hiding his real beliefs. Such a task involves looking at an important part of the *Guide's* introduction. Maimonides says that there is something that must be concealed from 'the masses', and also that the *Guide* contains intentional contradictions. My practice of taking him at his word therefore needs to be justified so, after explaining the ways in which those contradictions are often understood, I will present an alternative reading, in order to explain why I think that these purported proof texts are not concerned with Maimonides' 'real opinion' about theological doctrines. This is a contentious view: in Maimonidean studies, it is more controversial to assume that the *Guide's* author is sincere when he presents his opinions about theological issues than to assume that he was engaging in dissimulation. The present chapter therefore has a polemical aspect.

There was controversy over Maimonides' work almost immediately. During his lifetime, he was condemned by a religious leader in Baghdad for, on the critic's interpretation, rejecting belief in the resurrection of the dead. Resurrection is the last of the thirteen principles of faith that Maimonides lists, but there are occasions when he seemed to consider it a part of his general doctrine of reward and punishment. In subsequent centuries, there were two major 'Maimonidean controversies' in Spain and Southern France, which saw his supporters and detractors arguing over what counts as authentic interpretation of Judaism and its texts. Maimonides' attitude to philosophy was attacked and his philosophical bent has even been blamed for the decline of the Jewish community in Spain, with the claim that making human perfection dependent on intellectual achievement rather than fulfilling the commandments can weaken commitment to religion. José Faur takes the opposite view, pointing out that those who left Judaism tended to oppose philosophy, while followers of Maimonides retained their faith and defended it from anti-Jewish polemicists.[2]

Maybe this kind of reaction to his work was inevitable. After all, he spent much of his energy combating popular religious beliefs that he considered erroneous. It is possible that in doing so he unwittingly assisted the dissemination of those beliefs. Some claim that the kabbalistic tradition developed, or at least grew, in response to Maimonides' polemic against the very same ideas that the kabbalah elaborated. When he vigorously opposed certain beliefs that were present in the community but not widely promulgated in theological and rabbinic tracts, at least not explicitly, he brought these beliefs into the open, so it is claimed, and gave greater impetus to those who defended them.[3]

Kabbalah and philosophy are often presented as opposed to one another. Those who follow 'the philosophers' draw explicitly on 'external books', written by authors from outside the Jewish tradition, and seek a truth that is, in principle, universal. By contrast, the Kabbalah sees itself as based on a received tradition, although it can be creatively understood and expressed, and contains a kernel that would not be accessible had it not been passed down. In order to rescue Maimonides from the philosophers, he was sometimes said to have repented on his deathbed and embraced the Kabbalah. Nevertheless, there were Kabbalists who responded positively to the *Guide*. Quotations from or allusions to his works can be identified in kabbalistic texts. Even when they rejected his ideas, many kabbalists borrowed freely from him. One of the Kabbalah's major primary texts, the Zohar, alludes to sections in Maimonides' *Code*. It is usually dated to around the thirteenth century, and attributed to Moses de León and his circle in Spain, who probably drew on older traditions. Kabbalists themselves considered it to be the work of a second-century sage, Simeon bar Yoḥai, so they were able to take similarities between words in the Zohar and words by Maimonides as evidence that Maimonides was himself versed in Kabbalah. Also in the thirteenth century, Abraham Abulafia wrote kabbalistic commentaries on sections of the *Guide*, which seems to have gained some popularity. The practice of reading Maimonides as a kabbalist continues even today among some Hasidic thinkers.

A Hebrew philosophical tradition closer to the Arabic Peripatetics was also spawned to some degree by the desire to read the *Guide*. I mentioned in Chapter 1 that Jews in France wished to access Maimonides' work and, since they did not know Arabic, turned to him for guidance. While many, like Maimonides, left Spain in the mid twelfth century and moved East, others headed North. One person who ended up in Provence was Judah Ibn Tibbon, who was immersed in Arabic culture and literary customs. He put some Jewish texts into Hebrew for notable people in the local community, beginning a translation movement continued by his son and other family members, and earning himself the sobriquet 'the father of translators'. Many of the classics of Jewish philosophy are still widely studied in the Hebrew translations made by the Ibn Tibbon family, the *Guide* included. Translations were made of other Arabic texts as well, providing Hebrew readers with necessary background knowledge. As well as translating, the Tibbonites wrote their own works in various formats, and so an independent stream of Maimonidean philosophy arose, marrying Maimonides' instruction with lessons from other philosophers and also with independent thought. In this tradition, strictly philosophical treatises as well as many philosophical bible commentaries were penned.

Since Maimonides was already an iconic figure, the *Guide* quickly became a canonical text for Jewish philosophers. Commentaries on the work appeared soon after he finished it. And, because the *Guide* is written in a way that leaves it open to divergent readings, interpretations were almost immediately diverse. Some commentators were influenced by Averroes, whose own commentaries on Aristotle had great impact in their Hebrew guise. Averroes argued very clearly for a number of positions that differ from those that Maimonides promulgated. Perhaps the best-known example involves the question of creation. Averroes distinguished between the world's creation *ex nihilo* and the question whether or not there was an absolute beginning, a creation *de novo*. He argued that the world is created, since it is at all times brought into existence by God, but that it is also everlasting, and that there is no inconsistency in holding both to be true. Some claimed that Maimonides believed the same, that the world is both created and everlasting, even though he never explicitly says so.[4] It was held that since Maimonides was a great philosopher, he must have recognised true doctrines. When he appeared to hold a position that a commentator thought false, such as that the world began at some finite past time, or that creation *ex nihilo* requires creation *de novo*, he adopted these false opinions publicly but privately repudiated them. One of the major fourteenth-century commentators, Moses Narboni, clearly explains his strategy: 'his statements may be explained in such a way as to conform with the truth, and it is the task of the exegete to interpret the statements of the sage in such a way as to conform to the truth whenever it is potentially embodied in his statements. This is even more the case when the interpreter finds in some passages statements that openly conform with the truth, for this obliges him to understand some passages on the basis of others, to link them and combine them until they take on a single, homogeneous form that accords in general with truth found in a few passages.'[5] Such a methodology allows readers to take the occasional turns of phrase to be an oblique hint to a 'true opinion' in light of which the other passages ought to be understood. In an extract I quoted in Chapter 1, Maimonides himself writes that 'when reading a given chapter, your intention must be not only to understand the totality of the subject of that chapter, but also to grasp each word that occurs in it in the course of the speech, even if that word does not belong to the intention of the chapter'. Apparently in line with such comments, Narboni's principle allows for particular statements to be taken out of their immediate context and employed in order to support the claim that Maimonides believed something that he apparently repudiated. I will return to Maimonides' instructions below, when attempting to justify the claim that he is sincere when he presents his theological opinions.

Until now, I have touched on some of the interpretations that are better known in the English-speaking and academic worlds. There were also traditions of Maimonidean thought in the Arabic-Jewish world. This body of work is less familiar to scholars, so I cannot say exactly how extensive it was or still is. That which is now most widely known about is the Yemenite tradition; it flourished especially between the fourteenth and sixteenth centuries but could be said to have continued until the twenty-first.[6] Today, the *Code* is a main halakhic authority for the Yemenite Jewish community. However, Jewish Maimonideanism in the Islamicate world didn't necessarily correspond to an impact outside the Jewish community. Certainly, Maimonides' influence on Islamic thought is not comparable to that which he had on the Latins. Muslim philosophers writing in Arabic had access to the same works that Maimonides made use of, and it is possible that many would simply not have felt the need to consult the *Guide*, which was, after all, focused so greatly on explaining the Bible and the rabbis. Latin translations of the *Guide*, by contrast, presented Christian thinkers with a text that they found valuable in its own right, for both the exegetical and the philosophical parts.

Modern European streams of Judaism also found their inspiration in Maimonides. Moses Mendelssohn was the main progenitor of enlightenment Judaism and author of *Jerusalem*, a work that Kant misrepresents, probably deliberately, and criticises in *Religion Within the Limits of Reason Alone*. Mendelssohn was a prolific author and a fine writer, known as the 'Socrates of Berlin'. He counted Maimonides among his major influences, and was also associated with his medieval namesake by contemporaries for his fame among the Christians and his mastery of rabbinic texts. Although he objected to Maimonides' thirteen principles, since he wished to align Judaism with the contemporary conviction that religion is private and undogmatic, Mendelssohn followed Maimonides in arguing for the validity of Jewish belief and practice on the basis of universal principles. And, like Maimonides, Mendelssohn stood at a juncture in Jewish history. It was a time when Ashkenazi Jews were beginning to face emancipation, and the Enlightenment held out a putative promise of equality on the basis of universal, ethical principles. In pointing out that the pretensions to universality often masked demands to abandon tradition and neglect the individual experiences of those who did not already belong to the majority, Mendelssohn articulated a problem that would pervade modern European Jewish thought, the relationship between Judaism and a state-power imbued with the dominant Christian religion. Some argue that this problem is the lens through which medieval Arabic thought is often anachronistically viewed, and they include readings of Maimonides in that assessment.[7]

After Mendelssohn, German Jews gradually became increasingly integrated into society and Germany became the crucible for Jewish engagement with European Enlightenment ideas. Many philosophers looked to Maimonides as a respected authority with a universal reputation and outlook. For instance, the great neo-Kantian philosopher Hermann Cohen saw a kindred spirit in Maimonides. He argued that Judaism is, at its core, ethical monotheism and therefore aimed at the two points that Enlightenment thought held sacred. Judaism could then be seen to be the culmination of a rational religion in the same way as German culture and thought was portrayed to be. In fact, he argued, the Jewish ideal is exactly the same as the ethical and rational ideal that philosophers in the wider German world were claiming as their own. Since he viewed Maimonides as both a rationalist and universalist thinker, who insisted on a strict interpretation of monotheism, Cohen identified with Maimonides and interpreted his predecessor accordingly, emphasizing that the attributes of action with which Maimonides characterised God are moral attributes. Maimonides' religion therefore satisfied the demands of a truly modern and ethical faith. Not everybody, however, was in favour of Maimonides' supposedly hard-headed rationalism. Cohen's own illustrious student, Franz Rosenzweig, offered a more romanticised version of Judaism, one that not only emphasised the particularity inherent to people and traditions but also echoed Mendelssohn's objection to his contemporaries' pretensions to envelop all of those particulars in a universal theory. These philosophers are among the most important modern Jewish thinkers widely taught and studied today. It is worth mentioning that there were thinkers outside Germany who engaged in comparable projects of combining Jewish sources with modern ideas in various ways, including many in the Sephardi tradition, even if they are now less well known to the wider world, notable examples being the Italian rabbis and philosophers Leon Modena and Elijah Benamozegh. In the writings of almost all such thinkers, Maimonides can still be found somewhere in the background, if not right at the forefront.

Despite the occasional demurral, Maimonides also continues to be an inspiration for Jews with very diverse ideas about what Judaism should be. No doubt, his halakhic reputation makes interpreting him in a positive light attractive to some. For others, though, it is his reputation as a philosopher that motivates a creative reading. Nevertheless, the variety of interpretations are not alone responsible for the *Guide's* reputation as a protean text. The work itself is so rich that it lends itself to all of these different readings and you could argue that interpreting it in line with your own sympathies stays true to its goal. Maimonides presents readers with a guide to help them think through the difficulties they have with particular texts and ideas by giving them pointers to challenge and help them in their individual development. As José Faur states, 'the *Guide* demands an existential metamorphosis: in the end through their own hermeneutics, successful readers will become the author'.[8] Maybe the *Guide* could even be thought to explicitly invite tendentious readings in, for example, the following instruction: 'If anything in it, according to his way of thinking, appears to be in some way harmful, he should interpret it, even if in a farfetched way, in order to pass a favourable judgment' (1: Introduction, 16). However, Maimonides is here addressing people that he is discouraging from reading the *Guide* altogether, so it does not follow that he would have welcomed any interpretation that has him expounding views that anybody who happens to read it would consider favourably. Even so, the *Guide* has been compared to a mirror in which people see their own thoughts rather than another's arguments and ideas. The point is that, rather than reading it in order simply to understand what Maimonides thought, people ought to wrestle with what they find in the *Guide*: arguments, hints, proof-texts, difficulties, ambiguities. Doing so requires creative reading that forces someone to develop their own understandings of the rabbinic and philosophical traditions, and even reality itself, in the process of thinking through what they are confronted with in the *Guide*. The mirror needs to be polished, and working on it transforms the reflection.

One of the reasons that the *Guide* in particular lends itself to various interpretations is that it is an esoteric text. It is obviously addressed to a limited audience rather than to the general, Jewish public, and Maimonides makes few concessions to his readers, openly stating that the work cannot be understood easily nor without prior, relevant education. He often expresses himself laconically. In so doing, he can be seen to have adopted a recognised method that was able both to withhold certain matters from the uneducated, who would simply fail adequately to understand what they are reading, and to present readers with a test, ideally causing them to think and sharpen their understanding as they undertake it. Some of the methods he uses are familiar from Arabic works, such as using technical and brief expressions or scattering knowledge and explanations throughout the work (*tabdīl al-ʿilm*). In Chapter 1, I touched on the fact that it is also an attempt to replace face-to-face teaching, and the benefits that method enabled, when the *Guide's* addressee, Joseph, had moved away. A widespread method, and one that Maimonides probably used with Joseph, was for the student to read a text and the teacher to interrupt with remarks, corrections and extra information. Maimonides would have been able to judge his student's reactions, knowledge, and potential in a way that he obviously could not use to assess his reader's. Personal teaching can be tailored to what a particular student needs and adjusted as lessons develop. Replacing this dynamic requires Maimonides to write in such a way that forces readers to piece his pointers together without him spelling them out very clearly. He needs to find a way to communicate according to the various levels of education that readers will have. In order to do so, he presents a text that can only be understood if the readers follow the proper order of study, continue 'to learn everything that ought to be learned and constantly study this treatise. For it then will elucidate for you most of the obscurities of the Law that appear as difficult to every intelligent man' (1: Introduction, 15).

To a degree, then, it is uncontroversial to say that the *Guide* is esoteric. Unlike Maimonides' other religious works, it is not aimed at as wide an audience as possible. However, why and how he practised esoteric writing is disputed. Unsurprisingly, then, like the pious viewpoints, academic interpretations of Maimonides that try to read his work against the background of its historical context also diverge widely. Of course, academics are not free of ideological bias, and Maimonides' status probably influences their readings as well, but so do the varied styles of his different works and the unusual nature of the *Guide*. In the case of the *Guide*, it is often thought that a special methodology must be used to read it, one that might not be applicable to any other work in the history of philosophy. Others argue that all great works of philosophy must be approached with a similar methodology in mind, that throughout Western history philosophy has been written 'between the lines', only we have forgotten how to read it.[9] Depending on the scholar's inclination, the *Guide's* secret message might be that Maimonides was a mystic, a Spinozist, a Kantian, a sceptic, an adherent of an Aristotelian view that he claims to reject, a postmodern pluralist, or a humanist. These readings, one might think, are no less selective than the pious approaches that seek to use Maimonides as an authority to buttress their own views and approaches or as a springboard for creative theology. But even if that is true, there are also textual grounds to take all the different interpretations seriously, and any alternative reading needs to account for these reasons.

Whether the *Guide* is a reflection of a writing practice common in the pre-modern era, or whether it is unique, it is atypical inasmuch as Maimonides presents some unusual instructions about how it should be approached. As a result, much scholarship claims to find support for what is said to be Maimonides' secret message in the *Guide* itself, even though that message is never explicitly stated unless it is hinted at by an easily overlooked clue. His introduction includes directions to deciphering its innermost secrets. Almost invariably, academic readers use proof texts from the *Guide* combined with these instructions. Maimonides states explicitly that the book is not aimed at most people, but at the few who are capable of penetrating to its deeper meaning. In order to do so, he explains, they will need to connect disparate chapters, notice hints that appear out of place, and read other scientific and philosophical works that explain details Maimonides himself does not go into. I quoted the first part of the following passage in Chapter 1, but it bears repeating, together with its continuation, as an especially clear expression of the challenges facing readers.

> If you wish to grasp the totality of what this Treatise contains, so that nothing of it will escape you, then you must connect its chapters one with another; and when reading a given chapter, your intention must be not only to understand the totality of the subject of that chapter, but also to grasp each word that occurs in it in the course of the speech, even if that word does not belong to the intention of the chapter. For the diction of this Treatise has not been chosen at haphazard, but with great exactness and exceeding precision, and

with care to avoid failing to explain any obscure point. And nothing
has been mentioned out of its place, save with a view to explaining
some matter in its proper place. (1: Introduction, 15)

Perhaps most importantly, Maimonides says that there are intentional contradictions of two different sorts in the *Guide*, and that
they are there for good reasons. One is a function of teaching. 'For
there may be a certain obscure matter that is difficult to conceive.
One has to mention it or to take it as a premise in explaining
something that is easy to conceive and that by rights ought to be
taught before the former, since one always begins with what is
easier' (1: Introduction, 18). A teacher might use rhetorical or dialectical means, appealing to the pupil's imagination in order to help
them understand what is necessary for the more basic investigation.
'Afterwards, in the appropriate place, that obscure matter is stated
in exact terms and explained as it truly is' (1: Introduction, 18).

A possible example of this can be seen in the relationship
between physics and metaphysics. Physics precedes metaphysics
in the curriculum. However, although metaphysics is only studied
after physics, it provides the foundations for physics. There are
ideas that are explained and argued for in metaphysics that are so
crucial to studying the natural world that physics simply cannot
be engaged in without them. These include discussions as fundamental to natural philosophy as matter and form, the nature of
cause, universals, the difference between act and potency, and more.
Such ideas are introduced in physics but, instead of being investigated exhaustively, they are explained only insofar as is necessary
to understand the use to which they are put in the natural sciences.
Contradictions can arise in some cases, says Maimonides, once
the student has advanced further and is ready for a more detailed
account. Sometimes, the new information can contradict or appear
to contradict the initial lesson. Another example can be taken from
the *Guide* itself, and appears during Maimonides' discussions of
the planetary motions, in which he makes the following remark: 'I
did not explain to you when you read under my guidance, for fear
of confusing you with regard to that which it was my purpose to
make you understand' (2:24, 325). Teaching does not necessarily
involve explaining a matter at the utmost of abstraction. In order
to help someone to understand a difficult point, a teacher will use
concrete examples and metaphors to illustrate an idea, only later
expecting the student to grasp the overall point in a more general
and theoretical way.

The second sort of contradiction that Maimonides employs is the seventh and last in his list. It is especially important since it is usually used to justify hunting for hidden philosophical positions.

> In speaking about very obscure matters, it is necessary to conceal some parts and to disclose others. Sometimes, in the case of certain dicta, this necessity requires that the discussion proceed on the basis of a certain premise, whereas in another place necessity requires that the discussion proceed on the basis of another premise contradicting the first one. In such cases the vulgar must in no way be aware of the contradiction; the author accordingly uses some device to conceal it by all means.

Much of the secondary scholarship on Maimonides uses this as grounds to employ a method of reading the *Guide* that is today dominant in the secondary literature, even though it is increasingly being questioned. Literary and hermeneutical studies look for contradictions and seek hints that one of the contradictory statements is implicitly rejected. Often, readers assume that philosophy's teaching differs from that of religion and that when Maimonides asserts that there is an opposition between the Law and Aristotle, he is expressing the inherent opposition between the two sources. In these cases, his adherence to a more 'traditional' view is said to be only apparent. Maimonides therefore actually agrees with Aristotle on such issues as creation and divine knowledge, even though he explicitly criticises Aristotle's doctrines and opposes them to the Law. When he adopts an opinion contrary to that of Aristotle, he is motivated by the need to avoid scandalising the masses. Since these readings are so common among scholars of Maimonides and medieval Jewish philosophy, it is worth taking some time to explain them. Below, I will argue for an alternative interpretation of the way in which Maimonides employs this seventh contradiction, which I believe is not concerned to hide a heterodox theology.

There might be two different reasons for any philosopher to engage in such dissimulation. One is to avoid the persecution that, it is claimed, would inevitably follow the philosopher's public alliance with science and philosophy rather than religion or, at least, to avoid upsetting people and making them suspicious. The second is connected to Maimonides' endorsement of a scientific curriculum that is studied in a particular order, and only after someone has internalised the commandments and their benefits. It is thought that teaching philosophy to the masses would erode their simplistic beliefs, lead to them abandoning the commandments and, thereby, potentially, damage the fabric of society. These beliefs are then classed as 'necessary' rather than 'true', a distinction that Maimonides makes in the following way: 'In some cases, a commandment communicates a correct belief, which is the one and only thing aimed at – as, for instance, the belief in the unity and eternity of the deity and in His not being a body. In other cases, the belief is necessary for the abolition of reciprocal wrongdoing or for the acquisition of a noble moral quality – as, for instance, the belief that He, may He be exalted, has a violent anger against those who do injustice' (3:29, 514). On some readings of Maimonides, beliefs espoused by the Law, such as creation *de novo* and God's knowledge of particulars, are held to be necessary because they encourage people to behave in ways that facilitate the Law's aims, 'the welfare of the soul and the welfare of the body' (3: 27, 510). They are necessary but false; the true opinions are those that Maimonides attributes to Aristotle. Necessary beliefs can also include widespread opinions about what is good, such as that 'it is good to wear clothes', which contribute to acquiring good ethical dispositions. Recently, some scholars have argued that the *Guide* contains more incompatible streams of thought than these two. In order to account for their presence, Maimonides is then said to be presenting several different possible attitudes to religion, all of which are equally uncertain and equally valid in his eyes. He is then presented as a kind of pluralist thinker, open to widely divergent worldviews, hinting that the reader is free to choose any of the open possibilities.[10]

Such a view assumes that there are indeed real contradictions that cannot be resolved and, furthermore, that Maimonides would also have recognised that a resolution is impossible. I believe that neither of these presuppositions can be taken for granted. Assuming that there are irreconcilable contradictions seems a strange attitude to adopt towards philosophical texts. Much medieval philosophy begins with puzzlement over how it is possible that two statements appear to be opposed to one another when both seem to be true. A difficulty generated by an apparent contradiction or conflict calls for resolution. Frequently, philosophers would spend a good deal of time and energy seeking a solution that harmonises the two, showing that both can be true simultaneously in light of relevant distinctions and qualifications. Statements that are said to be contradictory might not turn out to be opposed if they are addressed in more nuanced ways. But, when reading the *Guide*, such reasoning is tacitly deemed unnecessary. Whether or not the inconsistency is real is a question that is rarely asked. The *Guide* is therefore often studied using a different methodology to that usually used when looking at other medieval philosophers. The problem is that insisting from the outset that two positions simply cannot cohere effectively blocks any attempt to think further about the issue in question. If they are unquestionably incompatible, there is no need to work out a solution to the philosophical problem raised. Instead, one can assume that there is no solution and the task becomes how to decide which of the two conflicting propositions one ought to prefer, if either, or, more commonly in scholarship on the *Guide*, which should be considered the author's true opinion rather than one that he adopts out of political expedience.

This criticism supports the general approach of those who read the *Guide* in a way that attempts to understand and expound Maimonides' explicit theological and philosophical claims. But it is a critique that could be turned on its head: the contradiction exponent can ask how her opponents can possibly know that a particular contradiction is *not* among those Maimonides intended and that are designed to be hidden from simple readers. How can they know that Maimonides did not make use of this kind of contradiction or that a particular inconsistency is not to be counted among them? Furthermore, since the *Guide* is not an ordinary philosophical text, and Maimonides announces that he will build contradictions into it, approaching it by attempting to reconcile the difficulties might seem to oppose the authorial instructions to look out for the contradictions. Indeed, Maimonides himself appears to rule out introducing qualifications or pointing to different contexts in order to resolve contradictions when he outlines the fourth in his list: 'There is a proviso that, because of a certain necessity, has not been explicitly stated in its proper place; or the two subjects may differ, but one of them has not been explained in its proper place, so that a contradiction appears to have been said, whereas there is no contradiction' (1: Introduction, 17). Adding qualifications or explaining one position in light of another seems not to be the correct methodology to use when reading the *Guide*, since Maimonides does not include this kind of contradiction among those that he says he will use. However, these are not the same as philosophical contradictions, as becomes clear when we consider that he tells us that it is one of the kinds of contradictions present in 'the prophetic books'. In doing so, he also reminds us of the *Guide's* primary purpose, biblical exegesis, by saying that 'it was with this [the explicit reasons that contradictions arise in the Bible] in view that this entire introduction was written'. This gives us an indication of how the fourth kind of contradiction is used. Maimonides is not signalling a condition or qualification that clarifies a philosophical argument but one that explains a biblical passage. Here is an example of such an apparent contradiction. 'Moses could not enter the tent of meeting' (Ex. 40:35) seems to conflict with 'when Moses entered the tent of meeting' (Num. 7:89). It is possible to explain that there were certain conditions that were not met in the earlier passage, and that they prevented Moses from entering. However, the apparent inconsistency is not pointed out in the biblical text, much less explained. Inconsistencies of this sort occur regularly in the Bible because of the equivocal terms used in scripture, and that Maimonides explains in the *Guide*. Therefore, the fact that the *Guide* does not contain the fourth kind of contradiction should not prevent his readers from introducing extra distinctions or qualifications in order to understand his philosophical and theological positions. Still, even if this fourth in the list of contradictions does not support a refusal to elaborate Maimonides' arguments by using qualifications that he does not himself make explicit, the question still stands. We might not wish to assume that Maimonides considered two propositions to be inconsistent, but nor can we assume that he would have understood how to resolve a difficulty using an argument that he does not explicitly promulgate. Nonetheless, it is helpful to think through various solutions in order to understand better what Maimonides did say, what he might have said, and whether the alternatives are themselves plausible explanations or reveal the limitations in Maimonides' own account.

Today, the name most readily associated with the form of 'esoteric' reading that looks for contradictory philosophical positions is that of Leo Strauss. The term 'Straussian' is used both in a positive and a negative sense. Those who follow a so-called 'Straussian' line consider him an inspiration, while those who object often dismiss his methodology and arguments as fantastical. Debates between the camps can be scathing. At the root of Strauss's interpretation lies the belief that philosophy and religion represent two different approaches to the world that are fundamentally opposed to one another. There can be some debate over whether one is more acceptable than the other, but no attempt to reconcile them can be totally successful. Strauss contended that this underlying clash has given western culture its vitality since, so he argued, western thought consists of the attempt to reconcile or balance the two which, although doomed to ultimate failure, has generated great creativity. In Maimonides, Strauss sees a classic case of this problem, which he termed the 'theological–political problem'. This is one of the major reasons that he considered Maimonides so important. Both Maimonides' importance, and the fact that his *Guide* seemed germane to the question that Strauss was dealing with, contributed to the impact of his approach. Strauss objected to 'historicism', considering it a sterile and unimportant pursuit that reduced the great texts and traditions to little more than museum pieces. In response to a question as to whether reading Maimonides through these lenses is an anachronistic hangover stemming from the Enlightenment concerns mentioned above in connection with modern philosophers, Strauss could both deny the charge and draw its venom by arguing that the question itself is misplaced. Maimonides was a serious thinker concerned with serious matters, and no issue is graver than that at the very basis of human nature. As with the approaches above that attempt to be faithful to Maimonides in their own, different, contexts, this could be considered an appropriate method of reading the *Guide* even by those who consider it ahistorical.

Strauss was a brilliant thinker and writer, and he noticed details in texts that escape most readers. His interpretations cannot be adequately addressed or summarised in a few paragraphs. Moreover, what is most important for our purposes is less Strauss himself but the fact that so many who write about the *Guide* today consider themselves to be following his lead. Strauss noted that the *Guide* is a dialectical work and a replacement for oral teaching. Recognising these features are a key to understanding the work as a whole and some have argued that the seventh contradiction is precisely a description of dialectic.[11] While dialectic is a crucial part of the *Guide*, I am not convinced that it explains the seventh contradiction.

In earlier chapters, I introduced dialectic and touched on how it is employed in the *Guide*. I explained its use in philosophical discourse, in particular to test theses and to teach. However, the main purpose outlined in Aristotle's *Topics* was to delineate rules and strategies for debating, and the aim in debating is victory. There are two protagonists. One must defend a thesis while the other attacks it, and tries to embroil the defendant in self-contradiction. The questioner offers propositions to which the defendant can either agree or disagree. If successful, the questioner will introduce a premise that the defendant grants, while remaining unaware that the premise opposes the overall thesis. The questioner will then be able to force the defendant to abandon the thesis, at pain of self-contradiction. Questioners benefit from a strategy that reveals a certain idea while concealing something that might reveal the line of attack that will be adopted later in the debate. They might present premises in a disordered fashion, in order to hide the line of argument, or add irrelevant premises to distract through misdirection. These tricks help to hide the contradiction from the answerer until the questioner is ready to spring it.

Such a debate sounds similar to Maimonides' seventh contradiction, with the masses in the position of answerer, even though the contradiction is, of course, never revealed to them. However, in the particular instances in which scholars claim to identify contradictions in the *Guide*, including those addressed in earlier chapters of this book, this kind of debate is absent. Instead, the contradiction is seen as an expression of the overall methodology that Maimonides uses, and there are thought to be contradictions throughout between religious doctrines and philosophical arguments. This approach grants the following disputed claim: religion begins with obedience, whereas philosophy begins with wonder and questioning; religion and philosophy are therefore inherently incompatible. With this presupposition in the background, it is possible to read Maimonides' contradiction in the following way. If Maimonides is presumed unquestioningly to have accepted the philosophers' views, his own arguments are then held to be merely defending popular opinion rather than his own beliefs. This is evident in the way Maimonides used dialectic to defend a belief in creation and other traditional beliefs such as God's knowledge. The role of dialectic is therefore to defend traditional doctrines from the attacks of the philosophers. Those who know demonstrative philosophy, however, will have no use for it. Philosophers do not need religious doctrines and understand that they are fictions.

This issue is of great importance, especially to modern European Jewish thought, but it does not follow that Maimonides was struggling with it in the same way. The idea is never expressed outright in the *Guide*. Instead, Maimonides consistently argues for the opposite. He argues that religion and philosophy can both lead to the same place, which is a pious reverence and understanding of what is within the capacity of humans to understand. In his work, he emphasises the importance of tradition and philosophy for one another, while pointing out the limitations of relying only on one of them. He makes no secret of his claim that there are doctrines that cannot be decided on purely philosophical grounds, since they do not admit of demonstrations either for or against. The uncertainty is not hidden. Moreover, there are some explicit doctrines that would seem just as problematic to a vulgar reader that are not hidden at all. Aside from those discussions considered in the present book, to which Maimonides adopts uncompromising positions, he attacks a number of activities that people of his time and place engaged in, thinking them religiously mandated, and many still do today. He writes that those who expatiate on composing long prayers and sermons ascribing characteristics to God are 'truly ignorant' and mentions that the vulgar incline to idolatrous 'ravings', like using talismans, a practice common in his milieu.

Maimonides engaged explicitly in intellectual polemics, not to mention political arguments, without holding back. As he writes, 'I am the man who when the concern pressed him and his way was straitened and he could find no other device by which to teach a demonstrated truth other than by giving satisfaction to a single virtuous man while displeasing ten thousand ignoramuses – I am he who prefers to address that single man by himself, and I do not heed the blame of those many creatures. For I claim to liberate that virtuous one from that into which he has sunk, and I shall guide him in his perplexity until he becomes perfect and he finds rest' (1: Introduction, 16-17). Moreover, while the philosophers employ the fifth form of contradiction, which is used for pedagogy and is also present in the *Guide*, the only texts that he clearly says use the seventh contradiction are rabbinic. Aside from the *Guide*, he says that it is used in midrash and raises a question over whether or not it is present in the Bible, saying that 'whether contradictions due to the seventh cause are to be found in the books of the prophets is a matter for speculative study and investigation. Statements about this should not be a matter of conjecture' (1: Introduction, 19). So, while there is no doubt that Maimonides uses dialectic and it is true that the *Guide* replaces oral teaching, I do not find the presence of dialectic to be a compelling explanation of what he is doing in the seventh contradiction.

If it is true that not all statements that superficially appear to contradict each other are in fact opposed, readers ought not to assume too quickly, when approaching a philosophical text, that they understand enough to identify such contradictions and rush to judge two statements incompatible. I nevertheless believe that it is important to respect Maimonides' claim that contradictions of the seventh kind will appear in the *Guide*, so I think it important to offer an alternative reading. But there has to be some criterion that allows us to say that there are indeed discussions proceeding on the basis of incompatible premises. How, then, can we go about identifying these contradictions? Maimonides describes the nature of the contradiction he uses, so an apparent contradiction might indeed be one of them only if it satisfies two conditions. One is that it fit that description and the second is that it must really be present in the *Guide*. Are there instances that satisfy these criteria? I believe so, and I think that distinguishing two different questions helps to uncover a possible resolution. One is 'what is Maimonides' true belief?' The second is 'what is Maimonides concealing through using the seventh contradiction?' I think that the answers to these questions are not equivalent. They are two different issues. It is plausible, and I believe true, that Maimonides employs the seventh contradiction, as he claims to, but that he is not concealing a heterodox theological position in doing so. If my suggestion is possible, there is no need to claim that Maimonides contradicts his explicit theological teachings simply because there are contradictions in the *Guide*. He does not use the contradiction in the context of his philosophical arguments but, rather, in the context of explaining biblical passages whose inner meanings are opposed to one another.

I want to suggest that Maimonides uses the seventh cause for contradiction in his exegesis of certain biblical passages that the rabbinic tradition considers to be particularly obscure and especially deep, and that Maimonides refers to as 'secrets of the Torah'. They are known as the 'Account of Creation' and the 'Account of the Chariot', terms that appear in the Mishnah and which became associated with mystical traditions. The Mishnah forbids teaching these in public. In the case of the Chariot, it forbids teaching it clearly at all, instead stating that only 'chapter headings' should be taught and, even then, only to someone who is capable of understanding alone. 'Even that portion of it that becomes clear to him who has been given access to the understanding of it, is subject to a legal prohibition against its being taught and explained except orally to one man having certain stated qualities, and even to that one only the chapter headings may be mentioned' (3: Introduction, 415). Maimonides says that the Account of Creation is associated with natural science and the Account of the Chariot with divine science, which is a term often used for metaphysics. Since these sciences are not taught to beginners but, as explained in previous chapters, are more advanced disciplines, it makes sense that they should be considered esoteric. Maimonides writes, 'do not think that only the divine science should be withheld from the multitude. This holds good also for the greater part of natural science' (1:17, 42). He also explains that they have 'been hidden because at the outset the intellect is incapable of receiving them; only flashes of them are made to appear so that the perfect man should know them. On this account they are called secrets and mysteries of the Torah' (1:33, 71).

Nevertheless, while the 'very obscure matters' that Maimonides refers to in the seventh contradiction are connected with these sciences, the contradiction is evident only from Maimonides' interpretation of the scriptural passages that are known as the 'Account of the Chariot', the most prominent one being the first chapter of Ezekiel. The problem here is that Maimonides presents his interpretation in a highly enigmatic way. His commentary appears, ostensibly, in the first seven chapters of the *Guide's* third part. They are extremely puzzling. He says, 'I shall interpret to you that which was said by Ezekiel the prophet, peace be on him, in such a way that anyone who heard that interpretation would think that I do not say anything over and beyond what is indicated by the text, but that it is as if I translated words from one language to another or summarised the meaning of the external sense of the speech' (3: Introduction, 416).

The vision of the chariot includes four beasts, each with four faces. Every beast has faces of four different species of animal. A wheel is beneath them, and they are ridden by a man. It is an awesome picture, full of symbolism and imagery. There is no need to enter into a full explanation of Maimonides' exegesis, but it is appropriate to explain briefly a couple of examples to show how his explanations require the reader to work independently in order to understand them.[12] Maimonides hints that the beasts represent the superlunar spheres, and he is able to indicate this without explicitly stating it. The first chapter begins with a comment that some people look like animals, 'so that one may see an individual whose face resembles that of a lion and another individual whose face resembles that of an ox' (3:1, 417). Maimonides goes on to say that this explains the four faces that Ezekiel sees in his vision: 'all of them merely indicate the face of a man that tends to have a likeness to forms belonging to these species'. Apparently, the explanation is simply that the beasts' faces were human, but it is not clear how this helps to make sense of the vision. Maimonides seems to have succeeded in his plan to give the impression that he simply summarises the vision. However, a reader bearing in mind his instructions to 'connect chapters with one another' might recall chapters in which Maimonides outlined a theory that there are four superlunar spheres. As I mentioned in Chapter 5, he writes that 'the number four is wondrous and should be an object of reflection' (2:10, 272). Additionally, someone versed in cosmology and metaphysics would link the comment with the spheres, if they are able to connect the dots, for the following reason. Maimonides' associating each face with a human indicates that there is something specific to the human form that characterises them. Since reason is the specific human difference, he hints that the beasts are rational. In the second part of the *Guide*, he explains that the spheres are also rational, and that this accounts for their motion. Furthermore, each of the spheres was considered to be a species in its own right, so the idea that the beasts are four separate species all of which have intellect is an indication that Maimonides interprets the beasts in Ezekiel's vision to represent the spheres, even though he never explicitly says so.

Maimonides points in similar ways at the manner in which he interprets many other details of the vision, by indicating that a particular word or phrase is worth paying attention to, touching on a matter that he explains in detail elsewhere, or pointing out aspects of the vision that can only be decoded with wider reading. Maimonides sometimes associates biblical characters with schools of thought he saw in his own time, as I mentioned in passing in Chapter 3, in connection with his interpretation of the book of Job. I believe that he did the same with Ezekiel, and connected the vision with a group known as the *Brethren of Purity*. Attending to all of the hints and piecing together sections from other chapters of the *Guide* is the only way to understand Maimonides' exegesis. He is thereby able to hide the meaning he assigns to the vision and only awareness of this other literature enables a full understanding of his interpretation. 'On the other hand, if that interpretation is examined with a perfect care by him for whom this Treatise is composed and who has understood all its chapters, every chapter in its turn, the whole matter, which has become clear and manifest to me, will become clear to him so that nothing in it will remain hidden from him. This is the ultimate term that it is possible to attain in combining utility for everyone with abstention from explicit statements in teaching anything about this subject, as is obligatory' (3: Introduction, 415).

The medieval cosmological picture might not seem to everyone to be a particularly exciting topic or something that warrants being concealed. Still, while the details of Maimonides' interpretation are not so important for present purposes, its suitability as a candidate for the seventh contradiction is. From the ways in which Maimonides presents the commentary, it is clear that he both reveals and conceals, uses hints and allusions, and hides his interpretation from the masses. He does the same when explaining other biblical passages, although in a less extreme way. In these cases, it is clear that Maimonides is indeed writing in such a way that, as expressed in the seventh contradiction, manages to 'conceal some parts and to disclose others' and uses a 'device to conceal' the contradiction from those who are unable to decipher the meanings he ascribes to the different passages. But where is the contradiction, and why must the masses be unaware of it?

In the medieval picture, the Earth is at the centre and the planets were thought to revolve around it in what are known as spheres. The chariot vision is interpreted to teach that there are four superlunar spheres, and that each one of them has a particular relationship with a single one of the sublunar elements. The idea that there are four spheres is strange in medieval cosmology. Maimonides writes that it was believed by some of the ancients. One of the *Guide's* commentators, Isaac Abravanel, claimed that it stems from Avicenna, but this seems to be inaccurate. Instead, it seems that Maimonides was influenced by Ezekiel's vision, and developed his theory of four spheres in order to explain why there are four beasts. It has nonetheless proved difficult for many. Abravanel argued that Maimonides' reading shows that he did not understand the vision at all and that his exegesis is neither consistent nor true to the text. 'He made it all up. Dust in his mouth!' One of the pieces of evidence that Abravanel says Maimonides misunderstood is precisely this idea that there are only four superlunar spheres. Abravanel argued that the beasts cannot represent the spheres because that would mean that Ezekiel was mistaken. Along with many other of the medieval commentators, Abravanel interpreted Maimonides to hint that Ezekiel made scientific errors, of which the enumeration of the spheres is one. Elsewhere in the *Guide*, Maimonides presents the more usual configuration, in which there are ten spheres and, in his explanation of the Account of Creation, he explains that the sublunar world as a whole is moved by their motions and the light emitting from them, in line with more common Aristotelian meteorological theory. 'The elements intermix in consequence of the motion of the sphere, and their combinations vary because of light and darkness' (2:30, 354). Abravanel thought that Maimonides also attributes another mistake to Ezekiel, which is that the heavens make music, a well-known view that Maimonides explicitly rejects (2:8, 267). Like the four-sphere theory and its connection with the sublunar world, this doctrine relies on there being intelligible harmony and calibration between the spheres, which Maimonides tried to refute in order to support his arguments that God creates through will and purpose, as I indicated in Chapter 4. If Maimonides really did attribute mistakes to Ezekiel, he seems to be opposing the prophetic vision to his own view of creation too. Overall, it seems that there are two distinct astronomical accounts in the *Guide*, and each represents a different understanding of how the world is influenced by the heavens.

If the medieval commentators are to be believed, it would be obvious why Maimonides would have hidden the conflict between Ezekiel's views and his own. He would not have wished to reveal openly that the vision often said to contain the deepest secret of the Torah is flawed. However, some might not like to think that Maimonides attributes errors to a prophet. Instead, they might assert that he is simply unsure about how the cosmos is configured. Since he cannot decide on the basis of reason alone, the issue becomes akin to others concerning which there is no demonstration. Therefore, he sees fit to use the explicit sense of the vision to interpret reality. The uncertainty could then be connected with what Maimonides terms 'the true perplexity' when he explains the astronomical problems that I touched on in Chapter 4. The problem would then be that our lack of certainty leaves various possibilities open. The obscurity of Maimonides' presentation can be put down to the fact that 'an explicit exposition of this knowledge is denied by a legal prohibition, in addition to that which is imposed by judgment' (3: Introduction, 416). For present purposes, it is not crucial to decide whether the alternative view Ezekiel espoused should be considered to contain mistakes, although perhaps he could also be defended by noting that the Talmud attributes authorship of the book to 'the men of the great assembly', a court that operated around the time the events in the book of Ezekiel took place, rather than to the prophet himself. Nevertheless, what is important is that the entire exegesis of this and related passages is presented in a way that satisfies the requirements of the seventh contradiction. His explanation of Ezekiel proceeds 'on the basis of a certain premise', while his explanation of the cosmos in other parts of the *Guide* proceeds 'on the basis of another premise contradicting the first one'. It is clear that the conflict is concealed because Maimonides' entire interpretation is concealed. The intricacies of the ways in which people understood the phenomena they witnessed need not be discussed here. However, it is relevant that the *Guide* contains two divergent explanations of them.

This is simply a small taste of Maimonides' explanation, and I use it merely to illustrate that there are contradictions built into his exegesis of different passages of scripture. They are well hidden and fit Maimonides' description of the way in which he uses contradictions. While this explanation might seem anticlimactic to those who would like Maimonides to be a radical who opposes religious ideas, his explicit doctrines are radical enough that there is no need to assume that he would have repudiated them. I believe that thinking about his arguments and claims in their own right, without wondering whether he is secretly a heretic, makes for far more interesting philosophical arguments. His introduction need not serve as a warrant to read these arguments by seeking hints that he did not consider them to be sound. Instead, it is possible to approach the *Guide* not only as a great literary composition but also as a serious work of philosophy that challenges its readers to understand its arguments and claims. And it is possible to do so while respecting Maimonides' instructions to pay attention to intentional contradictions, connect disparate chapters with one another, and attend to asides with more care than they appear at first sight to warrant. The *Guide* can be read without looking for opposition between its apparent theological and philosophical teachings and its author's 'true belief' about those teachings while, at the same time, taking his instructions about how to read it seriously.

Does this solution preclude the possibility that there could be others? Of course not. However, they must be shown both to be present in the *Guide* and also to fit Maimonides' description. Many of those who interpret Maimonides to be hiding his theological opinion assume, perhaps unwittingly, that Maimonides' *Guide* is not really a demanding work of philosophy at all. There are assumptions that he contradicted himself in elementary ways. Of course, he may have done so, and he might not even have been aware. But as readers of a philosophical or theological work, one cannot assume unquestioningly that what initially appears to us to be a contradiction is really a contradiction, nor can one assume that it would also have been considered a contradiction by the work's author. At the very least, it makes for an uninteresting methodology to use when studying the history of philosophy, since it allows readers to avoid a good deal of subtle and technical philosophical analysis. When faced with a text that is difficult to understand, we need not automatically assume that we already grasp the nuances of the author's philosophical ideas. And we cannot take for granted that Maimonides would have thought what we expect him to have thought. If he writes something that seems to be at odds with a preconception we have about what he ought to have written, that should provoke us to think the issue through further, rather than to dismiss his argument as feigned. Far from indicating that Maimonides slavishly follows other philosophical authorities, the *Guide's* literary character can be seen to allow for interpreting it philosophically in ways that reveal him to be a complex, exciting, and challenging thinker. This judgement applies not only to historians of philosophy or academic studies of Maimonides. While many of his scientific ideas are outdated, much of his approach is still relevant. His attitude to seeking truth and his commitments to philosophy and community continue to inspire. Following his lead through the *Guide* involves working through a number of issues of lasting concern. Maimonides' prompts and arguments have proved a fruitful resource for generations and there is every reason to think they will continue to do so.

Further Reading

Since Maimonides has been so influential and so diversely understood, plunging into the vast secondary literature is daunting and
choosing what to read can be somewhat arbitrary. Here are some
good places to begin and some fundamental studies, but the list is
far from comprehensive.

For general overviews, there are a number of helpful and accessible books on Maimonides. Two short introductions are Manekin
(2004) and Seeskin (1996), the second of which both introduces
Maimonides and argues that his positions remain relevant. Seeskin
(2000) goes into more detail. Rudavsky (2010) is an especially helpful
place to go for a survey of the many disagreements in current scholarship over how to interpret Maimonides on particular issues. Ivry
recently wrote a summary of the entire *Guide* (2016), which covers
all its parts and adopts an alternative line of interpretation from
that presented here. I justify my own approach in Davies (2011). *The
Cambridge Companion* (Seeskin, 2005a) presents some important and
widely studied aspects of Maimonides' thought. For the nature of
the *Guide* as biblical exegesis, see Diamond (2002).

Anyone who approaches Maimonides' philosophical work
is well advised to explore wider streams in Arabic philosophy
as well. Shlomo Pines' 'Translator's Introduction', prefacing his
translation of the *Guide* (1963), is still an extremely useful histo-
riographical essay, although much scholarship has taken place
since it was written so it is now a little dated. Stroumsa (2009)
continues his project in seeking Maimonides' sources. For the philosophical background, Adamson (2016), Adamson and Taylor (2006),

Lear (1988), McGinnis (2010), and Sorabji (1983, 1988) are highly recommended. Marenbon (2006) presents an integrated account of medieval philosophy as a whole, which can help further contextualise Maimonides' arguments. McGinnis and Reisman (2007) includes a selection of translations of important passages. These works can help students understand Maimonides' philosophy against the backdrop of the kinds of things he himself knew.

One of the first essays students are likely to come across is by Leo Strauss, 'How to Begin to Study the *Guide of the Perplexed*' (1963), because it is included in Pines' English translation of the *Guide*. It is not really an introduction at all, despite its title, but see Harvey (2020) and, for a general introduction to Strauss, Robertson (2021). Strauss' methodologies are divisive, although they have been extremely influential on studies of Maimonides. In any case, Strauss' essay is not an easy one to begin with, either to understand him or to understand Maimonides.

In addition to the discussions on the specific topics treated in the present volume that are also considered in the general books mentioned above, here are some more recommendations.

For Maimonides' relationship with the halakhic tradition, see Halbertal (2013). On his approach to ethics and the law, as well as the human goal and perfection, see Hartman (2001), Kaplan (2002), Kellner (1990), Kreisel (1999), and Seeskin (2001). There is a chapter on Maimonides' account of divine providence and the problem of evil in Eisen (2004) and for Maimonides' account of God's knowledge and providence, see also Davies (2020). On the doctrine of creation, see Seeskin (2005b). For God's existence and attributes, see Altmann (1953) and Manekin (1990). I elaborated further on the positions I espouse here on God's attributes in Davies (2011) and also recommend Blanchette (2003) and Miller (2002) for technical contemporary philosophical analyses that defend the doctrine of divine simplicity. The entry on 'Existence' in the *Stanford Encyclopedia of Philosophy* (Nelson, 2020) is a good starting point for these issues. On Maimonides' reception in the Jewish tradition, see Berger (2011), Diamond (2014) and Kellner (1986). For something of his influence on Christian thinkers, see Burrell (1986), Di Segni (2020) and Wilkes (2012).

Notes

1 Biography and Introduction

1 Cited in Kraemer (2008), 226.
2 There are contrasting takes on Maimonides' life in books by Herbert Davidson (2005) and Joel Kraemer (2008). They adopt opposite views on this letter and the question of Maimonides' conversion.
3 Diamond (2014), 3.
4 There is an illuminating discussion of the different ways scholars have interpreted these statements in Kaplan (2018).

2 Life and Humanity

1 Aristotle, *De Anima*, 2.1.
2 Aristotle, *Nicomachean Ethics*, 1.1.
3 Aristotle, *Physics*, 1.6.
4 Aristotle, *De Anima*, 3.8.
5 David Blumenthal (2009) is a current proponent of a mystical view. Blumenthal is also notable for his work on the medieval Yemenite tradition of Maimonidean interpretation, some of which seems to have followed a similar line.
6 Aristotle, *Nichomachean Ethics*, 10.4.
7 Aristotle, *Nichomachean Ethics*, 7.14.
8 Kellner (2006), 149–63.
9 Kaplan (2002).
10 Hartman (2001), 60.
11 Ibid., 63.
12 Ibid., 64.

3 The Problem of Evil

1 Al-Ghazālī (2000), 130.

4 Creation and Infinity

1 Pines translates 'put under great pressure' as 'violently rebutted'.
2 For further on creation in this sense, see Burrell et al. (2010). In the introduction, Cogliati writes that 'it is understood as the ultimate ontological dependence of the existence of all things upon God as its cause', 8.
3 Another alternative is offered by Charles Manekin (2008), who argues that Maimonides was not concerned by the issues that motivate him to prefer creation *de novo* in his early works.
4 These examples are taken from chapter 8 of a Logic Treatise that most believe Maimonides to have written. For a dissenting view of its authorship, see Davidson (2005), 313–22.
5 McGinnis and Reisman (2007), 64.
6 For fuller discussions of each of the arguments in favour of the alternative positions, and the individual responses, see Seeskin (2005b).
7 The wider context of the later passage is the question of evil, which raises the question whether God could do what is impossible, such as create a physical world without decay.
8 Pines has 'All these are points for investigation, which may lead very far.'
9 Rudavsky (2010), 73.

5 The Nature of Belief in God's Existence

1 Davidson (2011), 235.
2 Izutsu (1965).
3 E.g., McGinnis and Reisman (2007), 63–8.
4 For an explanation in the Arabic tradition, see Avicenna (2011), 96–7.
5 Aristotle, *Posterior Analytics*, 1.13.
6 Aristotle, *On the Heavens* 1.12.
7 Mayer (2001), 35.
8 Hannah Erlwein (2019), 111–42 argues that Avicenna did not take himself to be demonstrating God's existence but to be concerned with elaborating what it means to say that God is creator. Maimonides is using Avicenna's proof in precisely this way.

6 Necessary Existence and Divine Attributes

1 See Miller (2002).
2 For further on the importance of these consequences for religious faith, see Goodman (1999) and Seeskin (2001).
3 Kenny (2005), 194.
4 Aristotle, *Topics* 1.5.
5 Miller (2002) offers a particularly helpful way of framing the problems and defending divine simplicity, and I draw on his work in this section. He responds to a number of other philosophers, whom I will not summarise, since the purpose here is to explain philosophical assumptions held by many in Maimonides' time in the light of some philosophical concerns raised today, not to address current debates.

7 Diverse Interpretations and Disputed Instructions: Reading the *Guide for the Perplexed*

1 Shapiro (2004).
2 Faur (2003).
3 Kellner (2006).
4 For more on 'perpetual creation', see Haliva (2020), 157–72.
5 Quoted in Ravitsky (2012), 167.
6 Langermann (2001).
7 E.g., Gutas (2002).
8 Faur (1999), xi.
9 Strauss (1980). See further below.
10 Halbertal (2014); Harvey (2020).
11 Seeskin (2000), 177–88. Seeskin uses dialectic to disagree with Strauss, and I think he is right to do so. I concur with much of his analysis, and my disagreement is purely over whether the seventh contradiction is a description of dialectic.
12 I have pieced together the interpretation in Davies (2011).

Bibliography

When citing from Maimonides' works, I have referenced English translations wherever possible, and tried for the most part to limit them to useful collections that should be easily available. References to the *Code* are either to 'Laws Concerning Character Traits' or *'Mishneh Torah'*. Citations from the *Guide for the Perplexed* appear with part number, chapter number, and page number, in the following way (1:1, 21). The page number refers to the translation by Shlomo Pines, and I have noted when I depart from his interpretation. At the time of writing, Lenn Goodman and Philip Lieberman are preparing a new translation.

Works by Maimonides

Book of Commandments (1972). In Twersky, I. (ed.), *A Maimonides Reader*. New York: Behrman House, 424–36.

Laws Concerning Character Traits (1983). In Weiss, R. L. and Butterworth, C. (eds), *Ethical Writings of Maimonides*. New York: Dover, 27–58.

Commentary on the Mishnah [Selections] (1972). In Twersky, I. (ed.), *A Maimonides Reader*. New York: Behrman House, 387–423.

Eight Chapters (1983). In Weiss, R. L. and Butterworth, C. (eds), *Ethical Writings of Maimonides*. New York: Dover, 60–104.

Mishneh Torah [Selections] (1972). In Twersky, I. (ed.), *A Maimonides Reader*. New York: Behrman House, 35–233.

The Guide of the Perplexed (1963). Translated by S. Pines. Chicago: Chicago University Press.

References

Adamson, P. (2016) *Philosophy in the Islamic World*. Oxford: Oxford University Press.

Adamson, P. and Taylor, R. (2006). *The Cambridge Companion to Arabic Philosophy*. Cambridge: Cambridge University Press

Altmann, A. (1953). Essence and Existence in Maimonides. *Bulletin of the John Rylands Library*, 35 (2): 294–315.

Aristotle (1984). *The Complete Works of Aristotle: The Revised Oxford Translation*. Edited by J. Barnes. Princeton: Princeton University Press.

Avicenna (2005). *The Metaphysics of the Healing*. A parallel English–Arabic Text. Translated, introduced and annotated by M. E. Marmura. Provo, Utah: Brigham Young University Press.

Avicenna (2011). *Avicenna's* Deliverance*: Logic*. Translated by A. Q. Ahmed. Karachi. Oxford University Press.

Berger, D. (2011). The Uses of Maimonides by Twentieth Century Jewry. In D. Berger *Cultures in Collision and Conversation*. Boston, USA: Academic Studies Press, 190–202.

Blanchette, O. (2003). *Philosophy of Being: A Reconstructive Essay in Metaphysics*. Washington, DC, Catholic University of America Press.

Blumenthal, D. (2009). Maimonides' Philosophic Mysticism. *Daat*, 64–6: v–xxv.

Burrell, D. (1986). *Knowing the Unknowable God*. Notre Dame: University of Notre Dame Press.

Burrell, D. et al. (2010). *Creation and the God of Abraham*. Cambridge: Cambridge University Press.

Davidson, H. A. (2005). *Moses Maimonides: The Man and his Works*. New York: Oxford University Press.

Davidson, H. A. (2011). *Maimonides the Rationalist*. Oxford: Littman Library of Jewish Civilization.

Davies, D. (2011). *Method and Metaphysics in Maimonides' Guide for the Perplexed*. New York: Oxford University Press.

Davies, D. (2020). Divine Knowledge and Providence in *The Guide of the Perplexed*. In C. H. Manekin and D. Davies (eds), *Interpreting Maimonides: Critical Essays* Cambridge: Cambridge University Press, 152–70.

Di Segni, D. (2020). Early Quotations from Maimonides' *Guide of the Perplexed* in the Latin Middle Ages. In C. H. Manekin and D. Davies (eds), *Interpreting Maimonides: Critical Essays*. Cambridge: Cambridge University Press, 190–207.

Diamond, J. A. (2002). *Maimonides and the Hermeneutics of Concealment: Deciphering Scripture and Midrash in* The Guide of the Perplexed. Albany: State University of New York Press.

Diamond, J. A. (2014). *Maimonides and the Shaping of the Jewish Canon*. New York: Cambridge University Press.

Eisen, R. (2004). *The Book of Job in Medieval Jewish Philosophy*. New York: Oxford University Press.

Erlwein, H. (2019). *Arguments for God's Existence in Classical Islamic Thought: A Reappraisal of the Discourse*. Berlin and Boston: De Gruyter.

Faur, J. (1999). *Homo Mysticus: A Guide to Maimonides'* Guide for the Perplexed. Syracuse: Syracuse University Press.

Faur, J. (2003). Anti-Maimonidean Demons. *Review of Rabbinic Judaism*, 6: 3–52.

Al-Ghazālī (2000). *The Incoherence of the Philosophers*. A parallel English–Arabic Text. Translated, introduced and annotated by M. E. Marmura. Provo, Utah: Brigham Young University Press.

Goodman, L. E. (1996). *God of Abraham*. New York: Oxford University Press.

Gutas, D. (2002). The Study of Arabic Philosophy in the Twentieth Century: An Essay on the Historiography of Arabic Philosophy. *British Journal of Middle Eastern Studies*, 29 (1): 5–25.

Halbertal, M. (2014). *Maimonides: Life and Thought*. Translated from the Hebrew by Joel Linsider. Princeton: Princeton University Press.

Haliva, R. (2020). *Isaac Polqar – A Jewish Philosopher or a Philosopher and a Jew?: Philosophy and Religion in Isaac Polqar's 'Ezer ha-Dat and Teshuvat Apikoros*. Berlin and Boston: De Gruyter.

Hartman, D. (2001). *Maimonides: Torah and Philosophic Quest*. Stokie: Varda Books.

Harvey, W. Z. (2020). How to Begin to Study Strauss' *Guide of the Perplexed*. In C. H. Manekin and D. Davies (eds), *Interpreting Maimonides: Critical Essays*. Cambridge: Cambridge University Press, 228–46.

Ivry, A. L. (2016). *Maimonides'* Guide of the Perplexed: *A Philosophical Guide*. Chicago: Chicago University Press.

Izutsu, Toshihiko (1965). *The Concept of Belief in Islamic Theology: A Semantic Analysis of Îmân and Îslâm*. Yokohama: Yurindo Publishing Co., Ltd.

Kaplan, L. (2002). An Introduction to Maimonides' *Eight Chapters*. *The Edah Journal*, 2 (2): 1–23.

Kaplan, L. (2018). The Purpose of the Guide of the Perplexed, Maimonides' Theory of Parables, and Sceptical versus Dogmatic Readings of the Guide. In Haliva, R. ed., *Scepticism and Anti-Scepticism in Medieval Jewish Philosophy and Thought*. Berlin, Boston: De Gruyter.

Kellner, M. (1986). *Dogma in Medieval Jewish Thought: From Maimonides to Abravanel*. Oxford: The Littman Library of Jewish Civilization.

Kellner, M. (1990). *Maimonides on Judaism and the Jewish People*. Albany: State University of New York Press.

Kellner, M. (2006a). *Must a Jew Believe Anything?*. Oxford: The Littman Library of Jewish Civilization.

Kellner, M. (2006b). *Maimonides' Confrontation with Mysticism*. Oxford: The Littman Library of Jewish Civilization.

Kenny, A. (2005). *Aquinas on Being*. Oxford: Oxford University Press.

Kraemer, J. L. (2008). *Maimonides: The Life and World of One of Civilization's Greatest Minds*. New York: Doubleday.

Kreisel, H. (1999). *Maimonides' Political Thought: Studies in Ethics, Law, and the Human Ideal.* Albany: State University of New York Press.

Langermann, Y. T. (2001). 'Mori Yusuf': Rabbi Yosef Kafah (Qāfiḥ) (1917–2000). *Aleph* 1: 333–40.

Lear, J. (1988). *Aristotle: The Desire to Understand.* Cambridge: Cambridge University Press.

McGinnis J. (2010). *Avicenna.* New York: Oxford University Press.

McGinnis, J. and Reisman, D. (2007). *Classical Arabic Philosophy: An Anthology of Sources.* Indianapolis and Cambridge: Hackett Publishing Company.

Manekin, C. H. (1990). Belief, Certainty and Divine Attributes in the *Guide of the Perplexed. Maimonidean Studies,* 1: 117–41.

Manekin, C. H. (2004). *On Maimonides.* Belmont, CA: Thomson Wadsworth.

Manekin, C. H. (2008). Divine Will in Maimonides' Later Writings. *Maimonidean Studies* 5, 189–221.

Marenbon, J. (2006). *Medieval Philosophy: An Historical and Philosophical Introduction.* Abingdon and New York: Routledge.

Mayer, T. (2001). Ibn Sīnā's 'Burhān al-Ṣiddiqīn'. *Journal of Islamic Studies,* 12: 18–39.

Miller, B. (2002). *The Fullness of Being.* Notre Dame: University of Notre Dame Press.

Nelson, M. (2020). Existence. In Zalta, E. N. and Nodelman, U. (eds), *The Stanford Encyclopedia of Philosophy* (Winter 2022 edition), https://plato.stanford.edu/archives/win2022/entries/existence/.

Pines, S. (1963). Translator's Introduction. In Moses Maimonides, *The Guide of the Perplexed.* Translated by S. Pines. Chicago: Chicago University Press.

Ravitsky, A. (1990) The Secrets of the *Guide to the Perplexed*: Between the Thirteenth and Twentieth Centuries. In I. Twersky (ed.) *Studies in Maimonides.* Cambridge, MA: Harvard University Press, 159–207.

Robertson, N. (2021). *Leo Strauss.* Cambridge: Polity.

Rudavsky, T. M. (2010). *Maimonides.* Chichester: Wiley-Blackwell.

Seeskin, K. (1996). *Maimonides: A Guide for Today's Perplexed.* Millburn: Berman House.

Seeskin, K. (2000). *Searching for a Distant God.* New York: Oxford University Press.

Seeskin, K. (2001). *Autonomy in Jewish Philosophy.* Cambridge: Cambridge University Press.

Seeskin, K. (2005a). *Maimonides on the Origin of the World.* Cambridge: Cambridge University Press.

Seeskin, K. ed. (2005b). *The Cambridge Companion to Maimonides.* Cambridge: Cambridge University Press.

Shapiro, M. (2004). *The Limits of Orthodox Theology: Maimonides' Thirteen Principles Reappraised.* Oxford: The Littman Library of Jewish Civilization.

Sorabji, R. (1983). *Time, Creation and the Continuum: Theories in Antiquity and the Early Middle Ages*. Ithaca, NY: Cornell University Press.

Sorabji, R. (1988). *Matter, Space, and Motion: Theories in Antiquity and their Sequel*. Ithaca NY: Cornell University Press.

Strauss, L. (1963). How to Begin to Study the *Guide of the Perplexed*. In Moses Maimonides. *The Guide of the Perplexed*. Translated by S. Pines. Chicago: Chicago University Press.

Strauss, L. (1980). *Persecution and the Art of Writing*. Chicago and London: Chicago University Press.

Stroumsa, S. (2009). *Maimonides in His World: Portrait of a Mediterranean Thinker*. Princeton and Oxford: Princeton University Press.

Wilkes, G. R. (2005). The Virtues of 'Rabbi Moyses'. In Bejzy, I. P. and Newhauser, R. G. (eds), *Virtue and Ethics in the Twelfth Century*. Leiden, Netherlands: Brill.

Index